NEW VENTURE LAUNCHPAD

Second Edition

Kevin C. Cox
Florida Atlantic University

Roland E. Kidwell
Florida Atlantic University

Jason Lortie
Florida Gulf Coast University

Kendall Hunt
publishing company

Kendall Hunt
publishing company

www.kendallhunt.com
Send all inquiries to:
4050 Westmark Drive
Dubuque, IA 52004-1840

PAK ISBN: 978-1-7924-6664-9
Text alone ISBN: 978-1-7924-6665-6

Published in the United States of America

Essential support for the creation and production of this workbook was provided by FAU's Adams Center for Entrepreneurship, The Knight Foundation, and the expert faculty and instructors at Florida Atlantic University.

FAU
ADAMS CENTER FOR ENTREPRENEURSHIP
College of Business
Florida Atlantic University

KNIGHT FOUNDATION

PHASE 1

Introduction and Overview

I. Introduction to *New Venture Launchpad*

The information contained within and presented alongside this workbook provides a complete, comprehensive, and interactive guide and framework for successfully launching a new business venture. The purpose of completing this training is to launch a new business venture, or to *learn how* to effectively launch a new business venture (at a later time). As such, the format and design is *applied* rather than theoretical and therefore requires that the content, instruction, and overall approach must be *applied* to an actual (or imagined) business venture. This training cannot be effectively completed unless it is applied. Once the training is completed, participants may or may not choose to continue the venture at their own discretion—but the venture must be maintained, in some form, throughout the duration of the training.

II. Instructor Introduction(s)

-Presentation/interactive-

Instructor(s) introduction: Background, experience, Q&A (from the students/participants)

-Key Point-

Your instructor, who will guide you throughout this training, is an experienced, certified, and verified expert of the new venture launch approach and associated process. As such, the instructor can effectively provide expert insight, suggestions, and feedback regarding the systematic approach to starting a new business presented in this training. However, your instructor is most likely *not* an expert in your specific business venture, industry, product, service, etc.; he/she *is not* a consultant who can provide you with answers, directives, etc. that are specific to *your* business idea.

Questions?

III. Student Introductions

-Presentation/interactive-

All students (participants) introduce themselves during this interactive session. Feel free to share any interesting or notable characteristics about yourself or your background. If you already have a business idea that you intend to work on or to apply in this training, please take up to 1 minute to provide an overview of that concept to the group.

-Exercise 1.1-

Resource Assessment

Launching a new business venture is very challenging and will require the dedication of significant resources. The specific resources required will vary based on the nature of the venture, and various resources can often be interchangeable, or convertible (e.g., capital/cash can be exchanged for just about any other type of resource). Below are some of the more common resource categories (along with descriptions/examples), that have been identified as potentially useful for starting a business. Think about the resources you possess and add them below, particularly those resources that you believe to be the most valuable or unique (plan on sharing a couple of these with the class).

Skills (e.g., can provide a specialized service)

Knowledge (e.g., a specific domain/industry expertise)

Time (i.e., the amount of time you will allocate to the new business)

Experience (e.g., experience gained previously that can be applied to the new venture)

Passion (e.g., a cause, hobby, interest)

Capital access (i.e., the amount of money you can allocate toward the new business)

Physical space (i.e., ownership or access to a physical space)

Social Capital (i.e., personal network ties, and contacts and ability to access their resources)

Others (e.g., certificates, degrees, licenses, permits, etc.)

-Presentation/interactive-

Participants discuss two to four of their *most* valuable resources and why they consider them valuable. Also identify/evaluate any resource deficiencies that are brought up in the presentations. The instructor will attempt to surface these deficiencies in the course of the discussion.

Questions?

IV. What Is Entrepreneurship?

-Presentation/interactive-

The most basic and fundamental meaning of entrepreneurship is simply business ownership (entrepreneurship is derived from the root word entrepreneur, which is sometimes described as someone who owns a business). However, entrepreneurship can take many forms. Motivations, characteristics, and outcomes associated with different types of entrepreneurship vary. Use this interactive session and instructor guidance to continue filling out the table below.

Description of the entrepreneur	*Example(s)*	*Characteristics*	*Motivation/ Outcomes*	*Goal*
Part-time	'side-hustle' Hobbyist	Not primary occupation; limited scale, etc.	Extra income Passion/interest	
. . .				

V. Course/Training Overview

The purpose of this course/training is to provide a comprehensive and systematic approach for starting a new business. You can begin this endeavor without any idea about the business you will be starting, with a basic business idea in mind, or with a fully operational business you hope to grow. One purpose of this initial session is to determine precisely what you hope to learn, receive, achieve, etc. by completing this course. Therefore, we end Phase I with a final exercise designed to ensure that no matter what stage you are in the new venture process, we cover any specific content you hope to learn related to entrepreneurship and starting or growing a business.

-Exercise 1.2-

Additional Topics and Specific Interests

Briefly review the table of contents for this workbook (i.e., New Venture Launchpad Table of Contents). Now think of any specific topics, issues, or information you are hoping to learn about throughout the course and share them with the instructor(s). These topics can be related to what you see in the Table of Contents or can be other topics that you believe would enhance your capability to start or grow a business. Give this serious consideration as the requests that are not in the Table of Contents *will* be added to the course content if they are relevant to entrepreneurship/business ownership. (*However, don't worry if you think of something else later, we can usually add it to the course content at the appropriate time, but thinking about it now is best!)

Questions?

Appendix 1

Start-up Playbook: New to the start-up world? This is a great place to start to brush up on the basics.

https://playbook.samaltman.com/

This course will provide insight into the key steps needed to build a successful start-up. With key points on learning how to rapidly develop and test ideas by gathering massive amounts of customer and marketplace feedback, stressing the importance on validation.

https://www.udacity.com/course/how-to-build-a-startup–ep245

Suggested reading: *All in Startup* by Diana Kander

PHASE 2

A Scientific Approach to Entrepreneurship

I. Historical Approaches and Methodologies

-Presentation/interactive-

Entrepreneurship education and training evolved significantly over the 20th and 21st centuries. Early on, a common approach to teaching entrepreneurship and understanding how to successfully launch new ventures was to look at large, established, successful businesses and imitate their processes. On the surface, this appears to be a reasonable and rational approach: if you want to start and build a successful business, why not look to some of the largest and most successful businesses? This approach led to replication as prospective entrepreneurs were frequently advised to simply create a much smaller version of these large successful corporations. There are several reasons why this approach isn't optimal.

-Exercise 2.1-

Working in teams, consider some characteristics you know about large successful businesses and share them with the instructor/class. With guidance you should be able to quickly develop a comprehensive list. Then, consider an entirely new business. How do the characteristics, resources, circumstances, etc. of a new business compare to those of an established firm?

Established Businesses	**New Businesses**
Characteristics:	
______________________	______________________
______________________	______________________
______________________	______________________
______________________	______________________
Resources:	
______________________	______________________
______________________	______________________
______________________	______________________
______________________	______________________
Objectives:	
______________________	______________________
______________________	______________________
______________________	______________________
______________________	______________________
Other:	
______________________	______________________
______________________	______________________
______________________	______________________
______________________	______________________

Discussion: Given the evident distinctions between the two, discuss whether or not you think this traditional approach of modeling new ventures after large established companies would be effective for launching a new venture/starting a business. Consider why, or why not? Be sure to discuss functional organization and business plans as they relate to the discussion and contemporary approaches to entrepreneurship.

Questions?

II. A Modern and Scientific Approach to Entrepreneurship

The preceding discussion highlighted why approaching a new venture, or start-up, employing the same model/approach that large established companies use, is not likely to be effective. Established companies have fully developed configured business models—this represents the difference between the many facets of a business model being known versus unknown. Therefore, established companies are largely designed to execute/operate and enhance efficiency whereas start-ups should be built and designed to explore and search for a feasible and scalable business model. A business model refers to all the components required to establish an effective/successful business (and these components are introduced in the following section and covered throughout the course).

-Presentation/interactive-

For now, consider some of the information that established companies would already possess that new businesses would not. Consider how this information aids the success of established companies, and consider how this differentiates new ventures from established firms. Also consider how many "established companies" have failed or are failing over the last several years, e.g., Radio Shack, Borders, Blockbuster, Sears, Sports Authority, etc. and the reasons why these failures have occurred.

-Key Point-

Operating/growing a business is starkly different when compared to attempting to identify an attractive idea for a new business.

Questions?

III. Finding Answers and Applying a Scientific Approach to New Venture Creation

The preceding discussion revealed that in most instances new ventures in fact operate almost entirely in "unknowns" (e.g., customers, pricing, distribution, product/service design, etc.) whereas for established companies most, if not all, of the components of the business are known.

Starting a new business represents an exploratory endeavor that requires an entrepreneur to search for information and identify the answers to the many questions and insights about how to develop an effective business model.

Luckily, there is a widely established, well-tested, robust, and rigorous methodology that anyone can apply to find the answers they are looking for. Although anyone can apply this methodology, it does take some practice, and it can be tempting to skip parts of the process entirely. Let's review this approach for finding answers and compare it to alternatives, while discussing the various business applications.

-Exercise 2.2-

Process for Systematically Finding Answers

FIGURE 2.1 A Scientific Approach

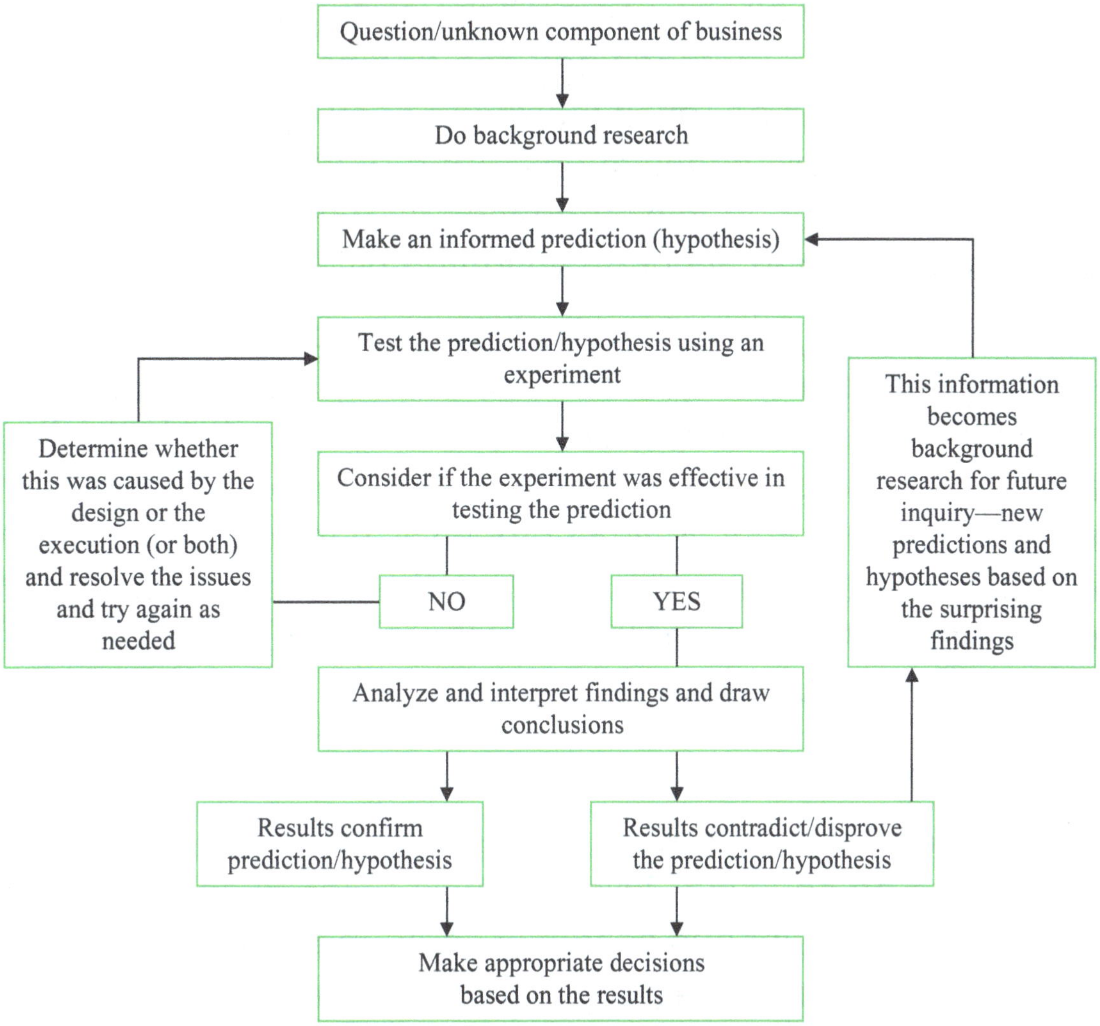

Source: Kevin Cox

You may recognize the preceding figure as it is a process you have likely seen before (perhaps when conducting an elementary or middle school science project); it is a variation of *The Scientific Method*. Now, you may be thinking—I'm trying to start a business, not give a poster presentation in a school cafeteria. Nevertheless, this is a *powerful* and *proven* process for identifying and answering questions as they relate to your new venture.

Only by applying this process can you ensure that the answers to your questions and associated predictions/hypotheses are accurate, empirically validated, and predictable. For instance, consider the thousands of mobile applications in the app store that have essentially no users. Skipping this process or applying some ineffective methodology for finding answers commonly results in reliance on (often incorrect) assumptions, unsupported intuition, or simply speculation—none of which can serve as an effective and dependable foundation for a new business. Instead, you need facts and accurate validated evidence.

Now, in Figure 2.2 consider the first and most pressing/important question or unknown you have regarding the development and validation of some component of your business. Fill in the first few boxes relevant to the question and how you will test/experiment to determine whether your hypothesis is correct. During this week conduct the experiment and fill in the remaining boxes to be discussed next week (and continuously throughout the course). Consider the key tips and additional points below.

-Key Points-

- Questions and unknown components of the new business venture can be *anything.* This scientific process can be employed for defining major and essential components of a new venture's core business model, e.g., product/service offering(s), or to determine minor facets on the periphery of the business, e.g., preferred logo design, website organization/color scheme, and so on.
- Background research can be relatively simple, or very extensive depending on the question you're attempting to answer. Sure, Google is a reasonable place to begin but also consider more specific databases designed for market research (e.g., https://steveblank.com/tools-and-blogs-for-entrepreneurs/#marketresearch).

FIGURE 2.2 Application to Your Business

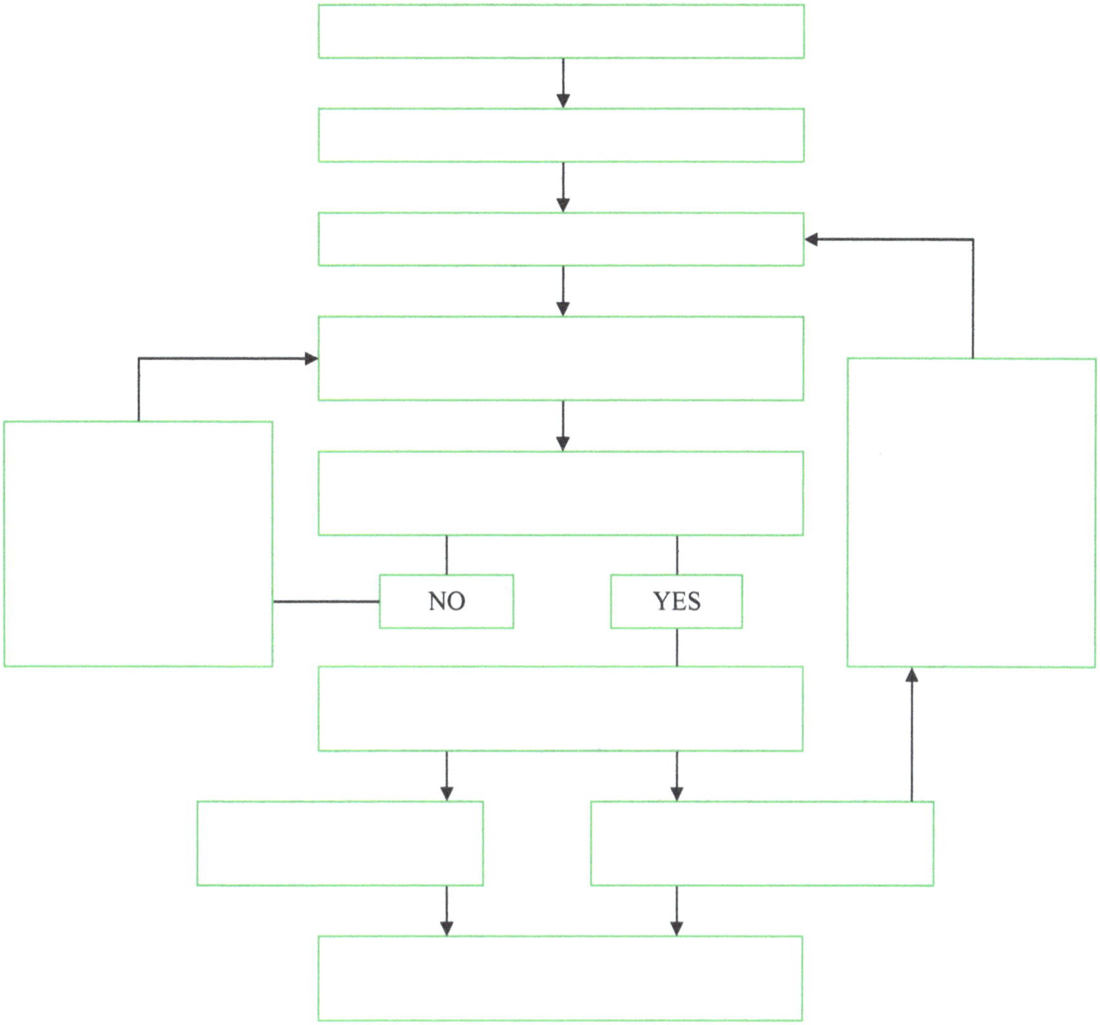

Source: Kevin Cox

- To ensure efficiency and effectiveness, predictions/hypotheses should be as informed as possible, intelligent, realistic, and logical. Setting up an experiment and getting results consumes time and resources. Making informed predictions will increase the odds that you will be correct, otherwise you may need to start all over again.
- Both *design* and *execution* are equally important in the process and failures in either can result in an inability to accurately test a prediction/hypothesis. Use care and caution in both design and execution.

- Interpreting and analyzing findings *must* be done *objectively*. The results should speak for themselves, do not embed any biases! If this proves too challenging, ask someone outside of the founding team to analyze the results.
- Assuming this process was executed effectively, make future decisions that are informed by and align with the findings. Too often, entrepreneurs ignore findings, which can be costly (especially those findings that contradict expectations).

Questions?

IV. Business Model

Although characteristics of different businesses can vary widely; all business models require certain essential components. Each component of the business model must be established and validated by employing the scientific approach presented above. A complete and comprehensive business model contains, considers, and addresses the 13 components shown in FIGURE 2.3.

V. Conclusion

The subsequent phases of this class will guide you through each of these components of a business model to ensure that an accurate and fully executable business model is established by the completion of the training. This systematic and extensive process can then be seamlessly applied to investigate, assess, and potentially validate any future business venture concepts.

FIGURE 2.3

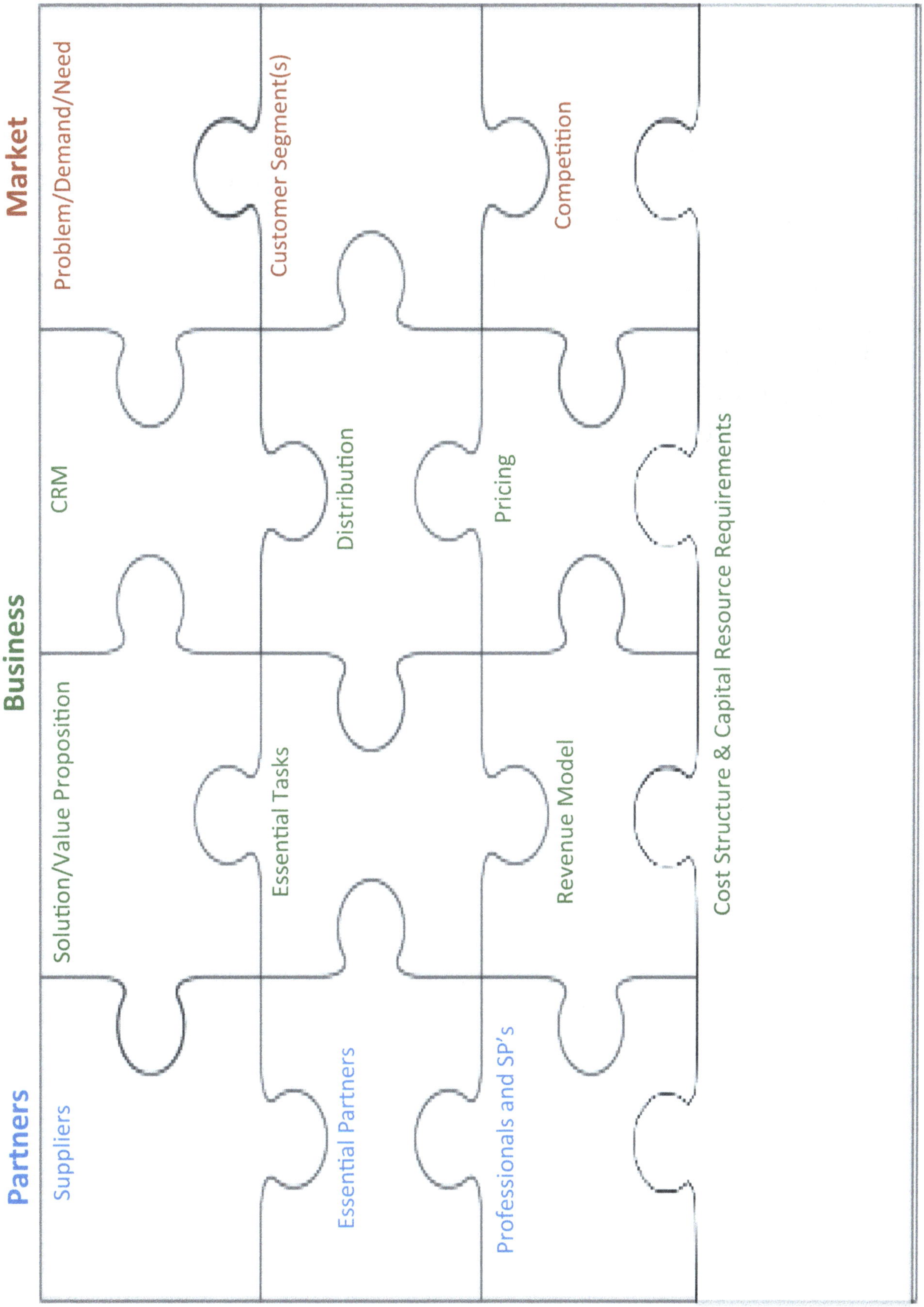

Source: Kevin Cox

Questions?

Appendix 2

This course will provide insight into the key steps needed to build a successful start-up. With key points on learning how to rapidly develop and test ideas by gathering massive amounts of customer and marketplace feedback, stressing the importance on validation.

https://www.udacity.com/course/how-to-build-a-startup–ep245

PHASE 3

New Venture Ideation/ Opportunity Recognition and Creation

I. New Venture Ideas (Identifying a Problem)

-Presentation/interactive-

Generating feasible new venture ideas can be simple, but also extremely challenging. Ideally, rather than sitting around brainstorming and speculating about wild ideas (which can be a fun and useful exercise for creative thinking and stimulating thoughts), you should instead identify a **problem**. Customers don't buy products and services in most cases, instead they buy solutions to problems. If you can identify a genuine problem and offer a reasonable solution—you've got a new venture idea that may very well be feasible. Finally, this approach helps to ensure that you will not build something that no one wants (which is the #1 reason start-ups fail). Think about the notion of problem solution as it relates to entrepreneurship and products/services as you complete the following exercise.

-Exercise 3.1-

Think about three products or services that you can buy today and the problem that they solve

Problem/Need	Solution (Product/Service)

Now identify three existing problems and *attempt* to generate a solution to them.

Problem/Need	Solution (Product/Service)

Discussion:

Consider the problems and their attributes in more detail.
Consider some interesting solutions.
Identify themes.
Consider how aware people are of the problem.
Draw conclusions.

Questions?

II. Unmet Demand and Other Perceived Needs

-Presentation/interactive-

Identifying a genuine problem and offering your solution to consumers is the optimal way to ensure there is demand for your product or service, and the best way to generate an idea for a new venture. However, there are other circumstances that are not traditional problems, and still result in a fruitful opportunity for a new venture.

- In some instances, a wide variety of market and economic factors can result in **unmet demand** for a specific existing product or service (or even an entire sector). Identifying unmet demand can require considerable and sometimes complex market and economic research. In other instances, identifying areas of unmet demand can be relatively easy. Referring back to Phase 1 of this process, not all entrepreneurship is technology- or invention-oriented or designed for a massive scale. For example, if you call most of the roofing, generator servicing, plumbing, etc. companies in your area and are consistently told they have no availability for 2 weeks or a month, you may have identified an unmet demand in your area. If you can perform or learn to perform the service, then that may be a great opportunity to form a venture.

Discussion: Consider examples of everyday entrepreneurs and implications of context specificity.

– In other instances, a new venture may provide a significantly **enhanced market offering/customer experience**. Consider the examples of Blockbuster versus *original* Netflix versus current Netflix. Each example addresses the very same problem/need yet offer considerably different solutions. This example also provides a few of the different ways significant enhancements can be achieved (e.g., convenience, price*, efficiency, distribution, etc.).

Discussion: Other examples and marketing implications.

– Fulfilling **perceived needs** can also yield good new venture ideas. You can probably think of many examples of products and services *you* consume that don't exactly solve a problem in a traditional sense, but instead fulfill a specific want/need.

Discussion: Example and implications.

– Fulfilling **future needs** can also be a fruitful source of new venture ideas. Social, regulatory, technological, structural, and many other types of environmental change can create an evolution in problem-solution scenarios and market demands/consumer needs/wants.

Discussion: Examples and implications.

-Key Points-

– Finding a problem is optimal for identifying a new venture opportunity. The nature of the problem matters though. The more severe the problem, the better the opportunity. Focusing on "hair-on-fire" or "migraine" problems makes more sense as opposed to minor annoyances.

– Consider keeping a journal of your challenges or common frustrations you face. These "problems" may represent an opportunity if you can devise an effective solution.

– Awareness of the problem also matters considerably, if the person who has the "problem" is not aware of it, is it in fact a problem?

- Note that all the other methodologies could in fact be framed as a problem solution, though some may not represent a traditionally genuine problem solution.
- Ensuring there is genuine demand for the "solution" you develop is essential, as most start-ups fail because they built something no one wanted.
- Most customers/consumers want to: make my problems go away, get me things that give me pleasure, make my life easier, meet my desires, meet my wishes, take away my pain, help me get things I want.
- Committing all the time, energy, and resources required to generate a new venture to solve a problem is far better than building something that no one wanted.
- The level of demand and awareness of the problem has considerable implications for many other facets of the business model.

-Exercise 3.2-

Opportunity Recognition Worksheet

For this exercise, write out the opportunity that you have identified. Don't worry about grammar or keeping it neat. Just get your ideas out there.

1.) What is the opportunity that you identified?

2.) What is the value your offering would give?

3.) Who are the typical users?

4.) Why would they use your offering?

Questions?

III. Value Proposition

-Presentation/interactive-

- The value proposition refers to specifically how your solution to customers' problem creates value for them. If the problem you are solving and the solution you are providing are genuine, then your value proposition should be relatively clear.

-Exercise 3.3-

Return to your examples in Exercise 3.1. Reconsider the problems and solutions that *you* identified. Attempt to clarify the specific value proposition associated with each of the solutions that you proposed. Once you have identified the value propositions, can you quantify them (e.g., how much are customers willing to pay for the value proposition/solution, or level of desire/need)?

Solution 1 Value Proposition: ______________________________

____

____

Quantification/Value: ______________________________

Solution 2 Value Proposition:

Quantification/Value:

Solution 3 Value Proposition:

Quantification/Value:

IV. Resource Assessment

-Presentation/interactive-

Now return to Phase 1 of this guide and consider in detail what unique and valuable resources you bring to the table that could potentially be leveraged to find a problem worth solving and to generate an attractive new venture idea. If any of the ideas developed during exercises 3.1, 3.2 and 3.3 appear viable, then consider whether you have any of the required resources for developing these solutions and/or how/where you might be able to accumulate the resources.

Because we all have a different set of resources, what might be a good business idea for you might be a bad idea for me. It is not just "how good the idea is" and how the market might accept it. You must be able to actually do it. For example, an idea to sell technology to power plants in China might be a great idea because it is a growth industry in a booming country. But if you don't know anything about technology, have no contacts in the Chinese government, or don't speak Chinese, it is not as good an idea. On a smaller level, importing products into a small Central American country might be a much better idea for a connected native of that country than it would be for someone else, all other factors being equal

Discussion: How resources influence idea generation, and viability; also, resource liquidity.

-Exercise 3.4-

Investigative Discovery Plan

For this exercise, you want to put yourself in the shoes of someone who is need and you are looking for what is out there that can help solve your problem. The goal is to learn what people have to say about what else is out there and how people's experience was using other products or services.

1.) How did you first come to recognize this opportunity?

2.) What are some existing products/services that are similar to what you would like to offer?

3.) Where can you find out what people think about other products or services that are similar to what you want to offer?

Social Media Groups/Pages:

Reviews:

People

3.) List questions you can ask to you learn what people think about existing products or services that are similar to what you want to offer? *Think recommendations and advice*

4. Join social media groups/pages and scroll through pages to see what people are saying. Then write down some keywords or phrases that stand out. Good and bad

5. Look at reviews of existing companies/products/services and list keywords for what people are saying about existing solutions.

6.) Go to those social media sites and ask your questions. Engage in the conversation and keep asking why, how and what. List keywords or phrases that stand out.

Questions?

Appendix 3

323 Start-Up Failure Postmortems: Afraid of failure? Find out from letters written by investors, journalists, and founders on what to avoid when launching your start-up.

https://www.cbinsights.com/research/startup-failure-post-mortem/

Remembering the Apple Newton's Prophetic Failure and Lasting Impact: Not all ideas are great, but they can lead you in the right direction. In this article, you will read about how the Newton came about and how it led to modern day technology.

https://www.wired.com/2013/08/remembering-the-apple-newtons-prophetic-failure-and-lasting-ideals/

After the Big Idea: Entrepreneurial Success Through High Performance Start-Up Teams: In this reading, you will find helpful tools and tips on how to work as a team and help your business flourish.

https://eiexchange.com/content/22-after-the-big-idea-entrepreneurial-success-throu

Exercise 2: The envelope exercise: This exercise developed by Tina Seelig at Stanford University will ask you to grow your initial investment provided to you.

https://venturewell.org/class-activities-inventor-entrepreneurs/

Want to start a start-up?: In this article, you will learn how to come up with ideas for start-ups as well as learn about the questions that arise, how to catch the upwind, problems and how to solve them and the design to wealth.

http://paulgraham.com/ideas.html

PHASE 4

Value Proposition Validation and Customer Segments

I. Validating Your Value Proposition

-Presentation/interactive-

Hopefully you've developed a general idea for a new venture that solves a significant problem or societal need. A general idea is perfect; there is no reason to attempt to create the entire business model immediately.

There's only one way to validate that your value proposition/proposed solution is in fact a meaningful and highly desired solution (remember, people want solutions to problems). Therefore, you must seek and receive feedback from *your potential customers*. But remember, you are not even sure who your customers are at this point because you have not validated that either. Find the people who *you think* have the problem/need associated with your new venture idea and seek feedback from them—depending on what they say, they may or may not be *your customers,* or may not experience the problem you believe they do. These are all hypotheses that need to be tested and validated (refer to Figure 2.1 to review this process). The easiest way to collect feedback from potential customers is to conduct interviews with them. Unfortunately, you probably will not be experienced or skilled at conducting interviews (initially)—but sticking to the following **rules/guidelines** will be immensely helpful, and your skills will improve quickly as you conduct more interviews.

Customer Interview Rules

- Collect as much contact information (name, phone, email, address) as possible/reasonable prior to interview.
- Request accuracy and brutal honesty above politeness prior to beginning an interview.
- Forget about nondisclosure agreements with interviewees.
- Forget about surveys.
- Ask open-ended questions intended to determine what the customer problem is and how important it is.
- Ask questions aimed to validate the problem/need; do not identify the problem/need yourself. Allow them to do it.
- Do not pitch your business idea/product/service to interviewees. *Never* mention your business concept until the interview is ending.
- If the interviewee does not appear to have the problem you are solving (i.e., they are not your intended customer), or need you are fulfilling, politely end the interview—you do not care what they think about it (unless they can identify another problem that you can solve).
- Be excited to hear things that you do not want to hear and that are unexpected and genuinely welcome criticism—this is learning!
- Listen considerably more (5 to 50 times more) than you speak.
- Focus on actual customer behaviors, past or present, rather than speculation about what someone would do. This relates to not mentioning your business idea up front.
- Attempt to develop a deep understanding of the problem and the task the customer is trying to accomplish.

- Always ask for deeper explanations about any seemingly meaningful information.
- Interview only one person at a time.
- Conduct all interviews in-person if possible; if impossible use Skype, Facetime, or similar technology to obtain a richer interview experience than would be gained by telephone or other methods.
- Record interviews when possible (audio and video) or bring a colleague who can make notes as you are conducting the interview. Either method will help you focus on the interview and recall what was said.
- You cannot conduct too many customer interviews, however once you have validated a hypothesis or are not receiving any new information you may move on.
- Ask each interviewee for an introduction to another potential customer.
- Write down and assess findings of interest immediately after the interview. Sometime later, return and reconsider the interview content for additional analysis.

-Exercise 4.1-

Draft a brief set of interview questions for your potential/hypothesized customers. You should include both good and bad interview questions. Keep in mind the preceding rules.

Good interview question 1: ______________________

____

____

Good interview question 2: ______________________

____

____

Good interview question 3:

Bad interview question 1:

Bad interview question 2:

Bad interview question 3:

Discussion: Present numerous examples of good and bad interview questions and analyze why the good are good and why the bad are bad.

II. Functional Prototypes and Interviews versus Behavior

-Presentation/interactive-

Interviews should be used initially to *validate* the problem/need. The problem should be significant and important. Until this validation occurs, there is no point in doing anything else, certainly no point in building something (hint: you do not know what your customer wants you to build). Only once the problem is scientifically validated (Figure 2.1 + interviews) should you consider dedicating time and resources toward building a solution or offering to fulfill a specific need.

Having reached this point, it *may* be time to begin building something, depending on the nature of the venture. But, how do you know what to build? Well again you intelligently hypothesize a solution/product/service, then you must validate whether it would be highly desirable to your customers. You can see how this could become annoying and inefficient, you build something, your customers don't want it, you build something else, they don't want that either and so on. . .

Luckily, in many instances, there is a solution. You can build the simplest and most basic prototype that minimally solves problems or even simply conveys the same features of your intended solution. This is often referred to as **Minimum Viable Product (MVP).** Here you can get creative. For example, rather than investing in a massive inventory of shoes, the founder of Zappos simply asked a shoe store nearby if he could take pictures of all the shoes, post them online, and if anyone bought shoes from his website, he'd buy them at regular price from the store. Apply these same tenets using minimal resources, and maximum speed. Many web- and application-based business concepts can be easily replicated using mock-up software or in some instances something as simple as a shared Google form/sheet. Remember the backend (algorithms, information, analysis, prediction, etc.) doesn't even have to work, it only needs to appear as though it does for you to achieve the feedback/validation you need.

An MVP is the *best* way to collect information from your customers and is far superior to basic interviews in terms of testing hypothesized solutions. Interviews are meaningful and important to establish and validate the problems/needs of your customers. But remember, in terms of information, behavior is far superior to interview responses, just as interview responses are far superior to survey responses. Observing what customers actually do with your product/service is obviously more accurate, insightful, and valuable.

Unfortunately, an MVP is not a viable option in every instance. Consider medical, food, and drug, and other highly regulated sectors, etc. For an alternative example, Appendix 4 includes an interview with the developer of a camera used for surgery. Also, check out the YouTube video about prototyping that provides insights and other options for these scenarios.

Discussion: MVP options, split testing, objective feedback, and other ideas and strategies.

-Key Points-

- If you cannot get any potential customers to use your (free) MVP, then it's either not a functional MVP or no one wants it. Either way, it is time to move on.
- The faster you can learn and react/evolve/make progress (i.e., iterate) based on customer feedback, the more progress you will make.
- Observe as much as possible, rather than interview, potential customers. If it is digital, you can track everything; in-person collect/record everything.
- Do not ask customers what features they would want or could be added, etc. They will always say yes to everything. Instead, wait until they identify and demand features that they claim are essential and not having them would deter them from future usage.

III. Customer Segmentation/Target Market

At this point, you should be able to determine more specifically your primary target customers. In fact, you should begin developing a comprehensive and sophisticated customer profile—the more you know about your primary customer, or target market, the better. In some instances, developing customer profiles can be relatively simple. For example, the customer may also be the user and simply a consumer (business to consumer—B to C). Or the profile might be more complex. Think about toys and other products for young children. Parents inevitably make the purchase but are not the actual users.

However, the customer profile can be considerably more complex and involve multiple people. For example, if the customer is another business (B to B) or a government (B to G), then there may be a distinction between the decision maker, the economic buyer (payer), and the eventual user. In some instance there may even be those who would benefit from not making a purchase from you! Your product designed for end users might put the decision maker's job in jeopardy.

Some customers can be very complex. For example, imagine that the customer for your product or service resides within a complex organization, such as a university (listen to the podcast in Appendix 4 to hear about some real examples and their challenges). There are also many instances where you may have a multisided market in which you have two or more distinctive customer populations to satisfy. Think about examples of platforms and marketplaces (again listen to episode 16 in the appendix). Finally, note that customers (and others important to the sales process), are *always* people, and you need to talk with and interview these people. Avoid falling into the trap of simply stating you plan to sell to schools, restaurants, accounting firms, the government, etc. Instead, determine who *all* of the people are within those entities who will play a role in the sales process, and start talking to them! If your customer profile is complex, make a diagram of it. If it is simple, then concentrate on developing more specific information about your customer.

-Exercise 4.2-

Begin with an example for the whole class then complete a diagram of your customer profile, include all actors who may be involved, and as much information about each actor as possible.

Discussion: Verified attributes about customers versus assumptions about predicted/hypothesized customers, where to collect additional information, additional considerations that arise during the exercise.

-Key Points-

- Your customer(s) are not a building or a group of buildings, but rather actual people with specific jobs, titles, and characteristics whom you need to interview, speak with, and sell to.
- You may have more than one distinctive customer segment, but unless it is a multisided market scenario where you need both sides initially, then focus on only one customer segment. Start with your *best* customer, identify your *perfect prospect*, and start there. Who is the one person, or type of person, who would definitely purchase your product? If you cannot sell to them, then there is a problem.
- Listen to your customers and ignore "insights" from anyone who is not your customer or involved in the sales process, including experts (and your instructor).
- Exercise 4.2 includes *all* hypotheses. *All* must be validated/verified using scientific/empirical approach (i.e., customer feedback/behavior).

-Exercise 4.3-

Stereotypical Customer

For this exercise, think in terms of who is the general person who will be the first to purchase your product or service. Think low hanging fruit.

1.) Would your product or service be for an individual or a business?

2.) Is the person that benefits from your product or service the same person that will purchase

If the user and purchaser are different, you will need to complete the this worksheet for each.

Demographics

Average Age

Family

Gender

Children

Location

Marital Status

Income

Role in Family

Any additional background information worth including?

Personality

Neutral

Introvert ○·····○ Extrovert

Analytical ○·····○ Creative

Cautious ○·····○ Curious

Organized ○·····○ Care Free

Passive ○·····○ Aggressive

Sensitive ○·····○ Secure

Liberal ○·····○ Conservative

Schedule

Circle when they would use your product or services.

Daily

Weekly

Motivations for Making Decisions

	1	3	5
Incentive	□	·····	□
Need	□	·····	□
Fear	□	·····	□
Power	□	·····	□
Achievement	□	·····	□
Affiliation	□	·····	□
Social/Societal Impact	□	·····	□

Goals & Challenges

What are they trying to accomplish when your opportunity would be used? What is their goal?

On a scale of 1-10 how difficult is it for them to accomplish the goal?

What is the impact of not accomplishing their goal?

What makes the goal difficult?

What conflicts do they face when they are in the process of trying to accomplish this goal?

What options do they currently have and what have they tried in the past?

Business Archetype

1.) What does this company do?

2.) Who are their customers?

3.) Describe the business model.

Roles

List the individuals within the company who are involved with making purchase decisions.

Role	Influence	Level of benefit from your offering

Have you called any of them?

Who is your in? *Who is the easiest person to connect with to help you get your foot in the door? (Think of them for the rest of the exercise)*

Schedule

What does their typical day look like?

Week?

What are important dates in their schedule?

When is the best time to connect with them?

Responsibility

Describe their role within the organization.

What does their job description look like?

Skills

Motivations

	1	3	5
Incentive	☐	···	☐
Power	☐	···	☐
Acknowledgement	☐	···	☐
Organizational Impact	☐	···	☐

Rewards

How do they & the organization benefit from your offer?

Goals & Challenges

What are they trying to accomplish?

What gets in the way of success?

How well do they understand the challenges they face?

What are their potential solutions for the challenges?

Have they used any in the past and if available why didn't it work?

Appendix 4

Shrimp Tank Podcast: In this podcast, you will get an inside look into Samyr Qureshi's and Adam Roth's experiences of being entrepreneurs in the education space.

https://shrimptankpodcast.com/ep-16-samyr-qureshi-ceo-of-knack-adam-roth-ceo-of-honorlock-2/

Talking to Humans: This book is a great quick read for extra insights on customer development.

https://www.talkingtohumans.com/

Focusing on Exercise 8: The Blindfold exercise: You will learn what it is like to walk in a customer's shoes. It's important to know that the customer does not know anything about your idea.

https://venturewell.org/class-activities-inventor-entrepreneurs/

https://www.youtube.com/watch?v=3sUozPcH4fY

In this podcast, you will learn about Marty Schultz and his current company, which builds audio/video games for the blind.

https://shrimptankpodcast.com/ep-19-marty-schultz-co-founder-of-blindfold-games-2/

Five Essentials for Connecting with Your Ideal Target Market on Social Media: This article will help you determine your target market by looking at your competition, and demographics.

https://www.entrepreneur.com/article/287192

How to Hit It Out of the Park with Your Audience: In this article, you will learn how MLB increased its ticket sales by appointing executives with excellent product market-fit knowledge.

https://www.entrepreneur.com/article/293019

How to Create a Customer Profile in 2019 [+ Template]: This template will help you decipher your perfect customer on whom you should target.

https://fitsmallbusiness.com/customer-profile-template-examples/

PHASE 5

Customer Relationship Management (CRM) and Competitive Landscape

I. Customer Relationship Management

-Presentation/interactive-

Now that you have identified *and* validated your (initial/best) customer segment/profile, you need to determine how you will manage the relationship with your customers. The question is, how do you **Get-Keep-Grow** your customer base? How is that process initiated, maintained, and enhanced/expanded over time? This process can also be referred to as a **Sales Funnel**, see Figure 5.1. The funnel depiction provides a good representation of the customer convergence/sales process. Consider your planned strategy for attracting and converting customers and complete the following exercise.

-Exercise 5.1-

Complete a diagram of your intended sales funnel. For example, consider how customers will become aware of the product or service. How will you find them, or how will they find you? Or both? Where? How many customers? Messaging? Promotions? Call to action? How much will that cost? And so on. Explain how you will achieve each of the processes laid out in the funnel.

FIGURE 5.1

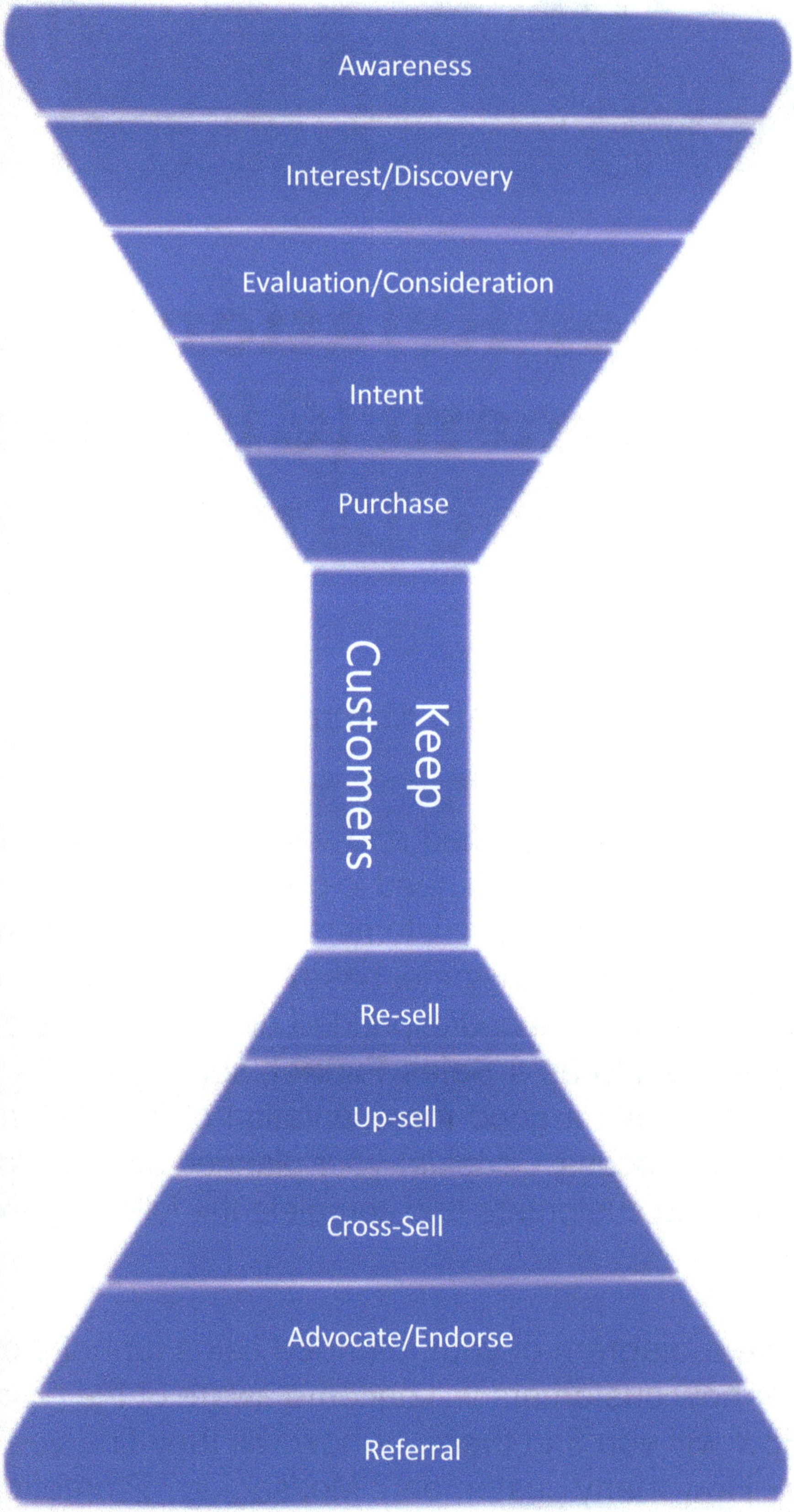

Source: Kevin Cox

Awareness:____

Interest/Discovery:__________________________________

Evaluation/Consideration:____________________________

Intent:____

Purchase:____

Keep Customers:____________________________________

Re-sell:____

Up-sell:____

____

____

Cross-Sell:____

____

____

Advocate/Endorse:____

____

____

Referral:____

____

____

-Key Points-

– Making customers aware of your solution/business can be challenging and expensive, not to mention getting customers to purchase from you. You need a good strategy and you *must* be solving a genuine problem or fulfilling an important need—if not, then the funnel will not function, and neither will the business.

– Consider, the parts of the funnel where customer may get "stuck." Try to identify why and alter the process to make it faster, easier, more efficient, and more seamless.

– Do *not* forget about keeping customers and making additional sales from existing customers or gaining referrals, that is, do *not* forget about postsale strategies and activities as they are important for sustaining the business. Keeping existing customers is always less costly than finding new ones.

– Exercise 5.1 includes *all* hypotheses, *all* must be validated/verified using scientific/empirical approach (i.e., customer behavior).

– Track every aspect of this process that you possibly can, and systematically analyze the data you receive from this tracking.

II. Competitive Landscape

-Presentation/interactive-

All ventures will have some competition from other ventures/firms. This is true even if your "solution" (product/service) is completely "new." If it's a good idea, then five other teams/ventures are working on it; if it's an exceptional idea, then there are probably 10 or more potential competitors (maybe many more). Also, very few things are genuinely entirely new. If you still contend there is absolutely no competition, then you might revisit the problem solution and the customer interviews prior to building anything because there is a significant chance that you are building something nobody wants (otherwise there would be some type of a solution/product/service already available, i.e., some competition).

Also, many competitors exist for your potential customer's time, money, and attention. Simply because you offer something unique that solves a problem does not mean there are no other competitors out there that present more compelling products that your potential customers will be more interested in purchasing, using, etc.

Therefore, while it's important not to get preoccupied with the competition (e.g., some business model prototypes largely ignore the competition), it is important to have a comprehensive understanding of the existing competitive landscape. For example, you do not want to build an inferior solution to a problem when a better (i.e., more effective, less expensive, or faster, etc.) solution is already available. It's always a good idea to conduct a competitive analysis. The easiest way to accomplish that is to set up a competitive analysis grid in the form of a spreadsheet. Determine which factors/characteristics are the most important for you to know about, and which might be the most important for your customers. For example, are your customers' price sensitive?

-Exercise 5.2-

Figure 5.2 shows a sample competitive analysis, with some categories/characteristics already included. Add additional categories that are important to know about your competition in comparison to your business venture. Then complete the grid (to do this, it is a good idea to switch to a digital version, e.g., Excel).

Discussion: Where to find information, types of additional information, why information is meaningful/important, strategies for outcompeting/differentiating, etc., product service life cycle (switching vs. adopting).

-Key Points-

- While understanding and being aware of the competition is imperative, it is important not to become overly preoccupied with the presence of competition. There is *always* going to be competition because customers have limited time, money, and attention, and your venture is competing with others for all three.

- In many industries, competition is not as cutthroat as it is sometimes presented. In fact, in many industries "competing" business owners often help one another by referring business, sharing information/best practices experience, etc.
- Don't be afraid to conduct interviews with the competition to gather information.
- Unfortunately lack of competition often signals a red flag rather than a Blue Ocean.

FIGURE 5.2

Company Name	Product	Website	Year Founded	Funding	Description	Launch date	Pricing	Features	Differentiation

-Exercise 5.3-

Existing Solutions

For this exercise, focus on what options they have for accomplishing their goal and what they have tried. Responses for whys and why nots should come from actual customers. Use their exact words.

Method 1

Business model

Why's/Likes/Pros	Why not's/ Dislikes/ Cons

Method 2

Business model

Why's/Likes/Pros	Why not's/ Dislikes/ Cons

Method 3

Business model

Why's/Likes/Pros	Why not's/ Dislikes/ Cons

Method 4

Business model

Why's/Likes/Pros	Why not's/ Dislikes/ Cons

Method 5

Business model

Why's/Likes/Pros	Why not's/ Dislikes/ Cons

Method 6

Business model

Why's/Likes/Pros	Why not's/ Dislikes/ Cons

Evaluating Existing Solutions

Why Likes Pros

What are the repeating reasons why people choose existing solutions?

Why Nots Dislikes Cons

What are some of the biggests reasons why people dislike or complain about existings solutions. Why dont they work?

Above are the things that customers are used to. If your offering does not include these things your customer will be dissatisfied and choose something else.

To the right is where you will be able to see if you have you have a niche or where you can find your niche.

Do any of the existing methods solve the problem?

If Yes, What is the biggest complaint?

If not, Why not?

Business Model

Rank the existing solutions based on business model. Which has the best execution?

	Solution	Differentiating Factor
1		
2		
3		
4		
5		
6		

Why did you rank them the way that you did?

What can you learn from the business models above that you can uss for your solution?

Offering

Rank the existing solutions based on execution from the customers perspective? Which has the best execution?

	Solution	Value Proposition
1		
2		
3		
4		
5		
6		

How does #1 have the best execution?

What is its biggest downfall?

Solution Development

Now it is time to take what you have learned and incorporate that into what you your business will offer.

Write out what your business will offer.

How does it help your customer reach their goal?

What makes your company different from the rest? What is the Unique Value Proposition.

What components from the whys/likes/pros will you incorporate to keep your customers satisfied and how will you do it?

How does your solution get to the customer?

How will your company make money?

How can you test this without spending any money?

Appendix 5

This software will help organize your sales as well as insights on the company, tracking deals and pipeline management.

https://www.hubspot.com/products/crm

This article summarizes the importance and the know-how of examining the industry where your proposed new venture is positioned.

https://www.entrepreneur.com/article/241074

What is Industry Analysis? In these articles you will find essential information regarding industry analysis and how it relates to a new venture.

https://corporatefinanceinstitute.com/resources/knowledge/strategy/industry-analysis-methods/

https://www.wallstreetmojo.com/industry-analysis-guide/

The Five Stages of Your Business Life cycle: In this article, you will read about the 5 stages of the business life cycle and how to move on to the next stage.

https://www.entrepreneur.com/article/271290

Lengthen Your Product's Life Cycle: In this article you will read about how to extend your product's life cycle.

https://www.entrepreneur.com/article/48722

7 Amazing Ways to Build Long-Term Relationships with Your Customers: This article will explain how to strengthen relationships with your customers and why it is so important.

https://www.entrepreneur.com/article/303911

PHASE 6

Channels of Distribution

I. Distribution Channels and Nature of Product/Service

-Presentation/interactive-

Distribution refers to how your product or service gets to your customers. There are many different ways products and services can be distributed. The options can be dictated by a variety of factors (nature of product, type of channel, industry infrastructure/established norms, etc.). Here we consider some of those factors and their associated characteristics.

Physical Product and Physical Channel of Distribution

Examples: cars, boats, air-conditioning units, wind turbines, shutters, and medical devices

Characteristics: These types of businesses can require large amounts of capital to massively expand (i.e. scale) and to cover overhead costs. Customer feedback is generally going to be slow, and selling is going to be somewhat costly (salespeople). This type of distribution is increasingly less common e.g., some cars can be purchased almost entirely online.

Physical Product and Web Distribution

Examples: Online retailers (Amazon, Zappos, WayFair, or Overstock)

Characteristics: Manufacturing, logistics, and shipping are critical elements of success; distribution may have low overhead. Customer feedback and development can be rapid if web traffic can be generated and achieved. This type of distribution is increasingly more common.

Web/Digital Product and Physical Distribution

Examples: Traditional enterprise software

Characteristics: Digital product may require physical installation. Distribution relies largely on traditional sales channels; customer development can be rapid. Increasingly more rare with the emergence of cloud-based computing.

Web/Digital Product and Web Distribution

Examples: Web-based and app-based services (Google, FB, Dropbox, or Kickstarter)

Characteristics: This format provides the fastest route to the customer and is the fastest way to acquire early adopters and receive direct feedback rapidly.

Discussion: Which of the above characterizes your business? What are some additional benefits and challenges associated with the types of distribution discussed above?

II. Selecting a Distribution Strategy

It's certainly worth considering how you would prefer to distribute your product or service if you could simply rely on your perspective to select the optimal strategy. However, as always, the only way to determine if that strategy would work is to get feedback from your customers. Remember, the way your customers want to buy your product or service is much more important than how you would prefer to distribute your products and/or service. Further, the industry infrastructure/norms may have considerable constraints on your options (and again, these can likely be attributed to customer preferences). Consider most foods and beverages, or pharmaceuticals. For example, imagine you create an energy drink. Sure, you could sell it online, and some energy drinks can be bought online. However, exponentially more—and the overwhelming majority of—energy drinks (and all single serve beverages) are distributed and sold in convenience stores and vending machines. Finally, you should consider geographically where you should sell. Is it all over the world, only in the United States, only in South Florida, or only in Miami?

III. Direct, Indirect, and Licensing

For most products, it has become increasingly easy to sell directly to consumers. For example, you can have a website and sell your products directly to consumers via the web and ship the products to them. Historically dominant traditional distribution also still exists where a manufacturer uses a distributor (wholesaler), and the distributor uses a reseller (retailer) from whom the end consumer purchases the product(s)/services. Generally speaking, the closer you are to the end customer (closer to a direct model), the more money or proportion of profits you will realize/retain. However, those models often must take on additional costs (overhead, marketing, etc.). The economics of the channels are important and should be considered, but in the end, the customers' preference is the most important consideration.

IV. Channel Incentivization

If you are selling through a channel, you *must* incentivize that channel. Otherwise it (they) will not make sufficient effort to sell your product. You must consider what will incentivize the sales channel (i.e. salespersons)? Money, along with valuable solutions for their customers, will work as well. Unsurprisingly, products that make the channels more money tend to be emphasized by the sales force. This can mean a high margin (commission) or something that is easy to sell (i.e., easy conversion, high quantity), or the best-case scenario, *both* profitable and easy to sell! To support and aid the ease of sale, you can and should consider providing training. You *should* know how to effectively sell the product from speaking with so many customers and being the company's first salesperson. You can also consider marketing to the channel about the product or service.

-Exercise 6.1-

Pick a product that you own (or product that you want to own). Now attempt to track that product to the original point of manufacture thereby diagramming the entire distribution process for the product. Consider the reasons why the distribution is organized the way that it is. Use boxes to identify every place the product travels beginning with its place of origin and use arrows to designate travel/movement. Be sure to include a description of how it moves and who moves it.

-Exercise 6.2-

Consider the material presented and discussed throughout phase 6 along with feedback that you have received from your customer interviews. Attempt to draft a complete diagram of your planned distribution strategy. Use the same boxes, arrows, and descriptions format.

-Key Points-

- The way customers prefer to buy/receive your product is more important than the way you would prefer to sell/deliver it. Listen to/observe your customers.

- Distribution can be very complex, and is obviously important. Consider all options. Experiment, and carefully consider various factors while keeping the customer experience central.
- There's a major difference between a distributor/sales team that pushes your product and one that simply lists your product on a sheet with hundreds of others—the difference is incentive, and sales versus no sales!

Questions?

Appendix 6

Distribution Models: In this article you will learn about distribution models and how they are beneficial to your start-up.

https://www.entrepreneur.com/encyclopedia/distribution-models

E-commerce Companies Eyeing Physical Stores to Up Sales: In this article, you will read about why e-commerce stores are partnering with brick and mortars and where it will take them in the long run.

https://www.entrepreneur.com/article/292763

PHASE 7

Essential Resources Requirements

I. Human/Intellectual Capital Resources

-Presentation/interactive-

Human and intellectual capital resources refer largely to the people you will need for your venture. You probably require a complete team to successfully launch a new business venture. Solo founding entrepreneurs are very rare (no matter what you might presume based on the popular media). It takes a team especially if you have *any* intention of raising capital. A one-person start-up presents unnecessary additional risk to an already risky scenario. For example, one person very rarely possesses all of the human/intellectual capital to pull off a start-up. Few people are good at sales *and* accounting *and* manufacturing *and* finance *and* legal *and* marketing and so on. But the business must be good at all those things. Sure, you can hire people, but they will not be incentivized and committed the same way as the founders. Think about it: Simply adding the right person to the team potentially doubles human and intellectual capital, and if you can find someone with more experience/knowledge then it is more than double the capacity.

Not only do you want to build a team, but you also want to build a diverse team in every capacity whenever possible. Think about the knowledge, skills, abilities, experience, etc. that you (or your existing team) possess and add people who have different knowledge, skills, abilities, and experiences. For example, if you aren't technology inclined, find someone who is (especially if you're trying to do a technology start-up!). Different businesses will require different types of expertise and experience, for any essential expertise required you might consider adding someone who possesses that expertise already to the internal team. Social, ethnic, gender, age, and economic diversity can also be beneficial (e.g., diversity results in different perspectives and experiences). How do you find these people? See some useful links in Appendix 7.

Once you have a team rounded out, then you can consider what other human capital requirements/needs you have. You may need employees, professionals, and vendors. This is discussed in more detail in the following phase.

-Exercise 7.1-

Use the table below to describe the characteristics of at least two distinctive and ideal cofounders. Think explicitly about your human and intellectual capital requirements.

Name	Years of Experience	General Background	Relevant Knowledge	Specific Experience	Skills	Other Resources	Other (personality, sociodemo-graphic)

Questions?

II. Financial Capital Resources

-Presentation/interactive-

Financial capital is arguably the most critical among the resources you will need to build your start-up/venture. This is the case because financial capital is the most easily convertible. Unlike other forms of capital, money can be (relatively) immediately converted into other resources (e.g., people, legal advice, a warehouse, or a patent, etc.). Unfortunately, it also has a tendency to be the scarcest in supply. You can read all about traditional (and other) new venture financing strategies, opportunities, and tactics in the **Special Topics in Entrepreneurship Supplement: New Venture Finance Debt, Equity, and Bootstrapping** (be forewarned you're likely to find some of the information disappointing). For now, it's worth addressing perhaps the most disappointing reality about one of the major misconceptions among nascent entrepreneurs.

[1]YOU CANNOT GET INVESTORS OR INVESTMENT WITH ONLY AN IDEA!

Investors do not invest in new venture ideas (and neither do banks). Investors invest in companies, yes, early-stage companies (in some cases), but companies. Investors do not invest in entities consisting only of ideas.

What can you do? You should begin by determining approximately how much it's going to cost to start this business. Consider strategies for bootstrapping and keeping expenses low (see **Special Topics** for details). Then figure out how you can get the remaining capital required. Family, friends, or cofounders may

[1] There is one scenario under which you can raise funding with only an idea, but it requires that you have a past 8–9 figure exit (i.e., you sold another company for 10–100+ million dollars). For more information, listen to the podcasts in appendix 7 to hear from those entrepreneurs who are in this enviable position.

"invest" (the term is used loosely) at this very early stage. Consider nontraditional financing strategies (special topics appendix). Finally, aim to start generating revenue as early as possible (double benefit: this results in financial capital and *may* prepare you for investors).

-Exercise 7.2-

Use the space provided to do a "back-of-the-napkin" cost estimation for your business venture. Think about all of the things that are essential for you to get your venture off the ground and have a product or service available for sale.

Expense Description	Amount
TOTAL	

Discussion: Consider the total amount and whether it seems feasible. Discuss the distinction between fixed and variable costs, and onetime costs versus recurring costs.

Now, did you remember insurance? Which types will you need? What about certifications? Licenses (city and state)? Benefits? Health care? It's likely you are missing some expenses. Based on experience with hundreds of start-ups, things have a general tendency to take longer and cost more than expected. Remember also that your start-up may be your only personal source of income, so include a reasonable salary for yourself. A good rule of thumb is to take the number above and double it. That may seem like a lot, but it is probably not overestimating the costs.

Discussion: Consider the *new* total amount and whether it seems feasible.

Questions?

III. Physical Capital Resources

-Presentation/interactive-

This category refers largely to the space and other supplies/materials you need for your venture. Luckily, much of the earliest work in most start-ups can be accomplished with very little in terms of physical capital (which saves financial capital). For example, customer interviews can be relatively inexpensive, etc. Only acquire physical space if it is absolutely necessary, otherwise avoid the overhead. If you do need space, then consider local coworking space or accelerators and incubators (also great places for networking, learning, and even finding cofounders). It's amazing what a few founders with their laptops, time, caffeine, and motivation can accomplish without much else (depending on the nature of the venture).

Discussion: Consider actual physical capital needs. Does this change your cost estimates?

IV. Relationship Between and Across Resources

-Presentation/interactive-

As discussed above, some resources are more or less convertible than others. Some may be of more or less value to your venture (e.g., if you had a dedicated space to work from, would that change anything?). Unfortunately, resources are not distributed equally, and therefore you may have more or less of any given resource (often less). Try to find local, or even national, support organizations that help entrepreneurs and small business owners (they are out there). Ask your instructor. These entities can be immensely helpful for new entrepreneurs. Finally, there is one resource that is generally (on a day to day basis), evenly distributed: *time*. Take advantage of that and use your time wisely. It's easy for founders to end up wasting time.

Questions?

Appendix 7

Cofounders Lab: This free website service helps you to find partners, collaborate and validate your ideas with other entrepreneurs along with giving you tools on your start-up business and helps with time management.

https://cofoundersslab.com/

YouNoodle: This start-up engagement site has a technology that is backed by a growing network of 200,000+ start-ups and trusted brand partners.

https://younoodle.com/

CodeArmy: This website offers many skills and educational materials to help turn your idea into a successful start-up.

http://www.codearmy.com/

The Changing World of Entrepreneurial Learning Resources: In this article you will read about how entrepreneurship is changing. It also includes resources to help further your business in today's world.

https://eiexchange.com/content/71-the-changing-world-of-entrepreneurial-learning-r

ShrimpTank: In this podcast you will learn about the founder of Squeeze, Elias Janetis, and his tech start-up. He is a serial entrepreneur with a lot of insights on today's start-up world.

https://shrimptankpodcast.com/ep-5-elias-janetis-ceo-founder-of-squeeze-2/

Shrimptank Podcast: In this podcast you will hear about Alexander Gomez and his company New Wave Endo-Surgery Inc. He is the inventor of D-HELP and founder of New Wave Surgical, which was listed in INC magazine 2014 as one of America's fastest growing private companies and the #1 fastest growing surgical device company. In 2014, DHELP was used worldwide in over 1 million surgeries.

> https://shrimptankpodcast.com/boca-raton-episode-69-alexander-gomez-ceo-and-founder-of-new-wave-endo-surgery-inc/

PHASE 8

Essential Partners and Essential Tasks

I. Partners and Vendors

-Presentation/interactive-

As presented in phase 7, you will require an array of human and intellectual capital to build your business venture. In this section, we discuss those that are most commonly required by entrepreneurs/founding teams. You may or may not need all of these resources and there is a chance you may need others not explicitly discussed here.

Suppliers

You may not think of your suppliers as partners because you are their customer rather than partner in a traditional sense. However, thinking of any suppliers you need as partners can be a very beneficial way to approach, frame, and maintain a successful relationship over time. This is especially true when using international suppliers. Contracts between two companies in two different countries can be notoriously difficult to enforce due to language and governance issues, and regulatory differences in domestic and international law. This is so much the case that once an entrepreneur pays all of the attorneys and other expenses, it may not be worth the fight to enforce a contract (even if it was financially affordable). Instead, maintaining a healthy relationship (partnership) can be more efficient. Further, in a sense, you are partners, whether it is raw material or finished products being supplied. Generally speaking, if you sell more, they sell more, you make more money, they make more money and vice versa.

Professionals

You may need to rely on professionals for specific services. For example, you may need legal help from either a corporate or IP attorney (or both) or a specialist in some other facet of law. You might need some type of consultant or paid advisor, or accountant (once you start making money) or bookkeeper, etc. These professional services can get expensive, so, early on, pursue only essential services. Also, while they are expensive, it is generally more expensive to have the services done in-house (e.g., hiring a full-time attorney for the business), so wait as long as it makes financial and operational sense to continue to outsource professional services.

Service Providers/Vendors

You might still need other service providers in addition to professionals. This could be anything, depending on the nature of your business. For example, will you have a fleet of cars/trucks that require maintenance? Or employee uniforms you need laundered to keep looking sharp? Office cleaning? Again, these relationships could involve anything depending on the business. Luckily most expenses come at a later stage.

Distributors

Distribution was covered in phase 6, but it's worth mentioning again here. Realize there is a cost associated with any type of distribution. You should shop all of your options, but again make sure the method you "choose" is also the preferred experience of your customers. Different distribution channels have different characteristics, outcomes, experiences, and costs.

Partners, Professionals, Vendors and Distributors	When Needed	Amount
TOTAL		

-Exercise 8.1-

Consider all of the potential, partners, professionals, vendors, and distributors you will require, at what stage and to what extent you will require them.

Discussion: Now consider all of the required additional human/intellectual capital listed here. Does this influence your response to exercise 7.2? If the start-up cost projections have increased from 7.2, reconsider feasibility with the additional costs estimated here.

Questions?

II. Essential Operational Tasks

All ventures have certain tasks and activities that are essential to the continued development and growth of the venture i.e., things that need to be accomplished. Otherwise the venture would be in jeopardy of failing. Obviously, you need to be aware of these operational essentials. A great way to get a handle on these operational tasks is to establish specific (SMART) goals, and determine what will be required to achieve those goals. Use Exercise 8.2 to establish some of those goals.

-Exercise 8.2-

Write down several specific, measurable, difficult yet attainable goals for the first 12 months of operation as follows:

3-Months

6-Months

9-Months

1-Year

Questions?

Appendix 8

CASE STUDY: General Mills Leverages External Partnerships To Grow Its Convenience Business Through Innovation: In this case study, you will read about how partnerships can help both parties—and drive sales.

https://cstoredecisions.com/2014/01/21/case-study-general-mills-leverages-external-partnerships-grow-convenience-business-innovation/

PHASE 9

Expenses, Revenue Model, and Cash Flow Generation

I. Types of Revenue Models

-Presentation/interactive-

There are many different ways that business ventures can generate revenue, that is, make money, some are simple and others are much more complex. Exercise 9.1 presents a number of common revenue models. See if you can figure what these descriptions mean and then come up with an example of a company that uses that specific type of revenue model.

-Exercise 9.1-

Product/Service Sale: ______________________________

____

____

Example: ______________________________

Rental/leasing:

Example:

Subscription:

Example:

Membership:

Example:

Freemium:

Example:

Advertising/referral: ____

____

____

Example: ____

Users (data): ____

____

____

Example: ____

Licensing: ____

____

____

Example: ____

Sponsor/Donation: ____

____

____

Example: ____

Discussion: Consider the various features (both positive and negative) associated with the different revenue models. Decide what revenue model(s) make the most sense for your business venture.

II. Revenue Sources, Stream Management, and Pricing

Many businesses generate revenue from multiple sources, which is great and generally attractive to investors. If this is the case for your business model, keep in mind that each additional revenue source may have a distinctive and unique revenue model (e.g., revenue model for customers vs. advertisers may look very different). Also keep in mind that each source will need to be managed as each is a distinctive customer who must be acquired. Recall that when we covered distribution channels and customer segments, it was strongly suggested that initially you should probably focus on only one customer segment and only one channel for distribution. This is also true for sources of revenue/revenue streams. Focus on one source of revenue. Once it is established and well managed then consider expanding to additional sources of revenue (in most cases).

It's important not to confuse revenue model with pricing strategy/tactics—these two are quite different. Pricing is simple: how much is the customer willing to pay? Pricing does not explicitly consider the revenue model but obviously has a significant effect on revenue. In fact, determining the optimal pricing technique can be very complex and should be approached scientifically, such that the combination of the pricing tactic and revenue model maximizes the revenue generated by your business model. This can be very tricky. However, once you have customers, it becomes relatively easy to experiment with various options. Use Exercise 9.2 to develop a better understanding of common pricing techniques and revenue models.

-Exercise 9.2-

Consider some examples of various products and services you are familiar with and add them into the table below, then determine the price and revenue model associated with each.

Household product	Price	Revenue model
Personal care product		
Service		
Software		
Mobile app		
Web service		
Fitness		
Content provider		

III. Expenses and Cash Flow Management

-Presentation/interactive-

A founder's major on-going concern is the amount of cash the new venture has on hand. This cash must be sufficient to meet short-term obligations such as employee salaries and benefits, rent, electric bills, insurance, and so on. Reaching breakeven and profit are important but as many have said, "Cash is king." Cash is the lifeblood of the business and it serves to pay the venture's expenses. A firm that is out of cash is out of business.

Getting a handle on periodic and one-time expenses is extremely important; review what you listed regarding expenses in Exercise 7.2. On the other side of the equation, generating a predictable and regular revenue stream is crucial. At the start, it is less essential to make a profit than it is to generate a plan to ensure enough cash is available to pay the bills. Make a list of one-time start-up expenses, then identify your revenue sources. Finally generate a list of monthly/recurring expenses. Putting a pro forma budget together is a good idea, but the most important element is sticking to it and adjusting as conditions change in real time. See the special topics appendix on bootstrapping as it provides some ideas on cash flow management. Pay no bills before they are due, generate invoices and bill customers immediately, offer discounts for early payment, collect a deposit up front, collect periodic payments if it is a long-term project or service. The main idea is to keep cash flowing in sufficiently to be able to pay your bills; also develop a 3 to 6 month cash reserve that will help you through any lean months.

In conducting financial analyses/estimations/projections, it is important to understand the difference between fixed and variable costs along with some other basic accounting functions and terminology. **Fixed Costs** are those that remain the same regardless of sales. For example, you will have the same (or similar) fixed costs for a given period even if you have no sales at all. Common examples would include rent, insurance, utilities, salaries.

-Exercise 9.3-

Estimate your Fixed Costs. Take a moment to think about all the recurring/consistent costs your business will have on a monthly basis. Either determine the actual costs, or a good estimation of each of those expenses and include a description and amount in the table below. The total represents the total amount of fixed costs your business should expect to have.

Description of Fixed Costs	Amount
TOTAL:	

Variable Costs on the other hand are the production costs per unit (unit may refer to goods/products or services or combinations of both). Variable costs include *everything* required to produce one unit of the product/service (e.g., do not forget to include the value of your time). The total sum of each of the variable costs required for production is important to know as this represents the total **Cost of Goods Sold (COGS).**

Knowing and understanding the COGS is important because this determines your **Gross Profit**. Gross profit is calculated by subtracting the COGS from the sales of the product/service.

-Exercise 9.4-

Estimate your Gross Profit Margin. Consider everything that it will take to produce one unit of your product or service. Now, use the table below to estimate the costs of all of those expenses (all of the variable costs). Then subtract that amount from the price you are charging your customers per unit—resulting in your gross profit margin.

Description of Variable Costs	Amount
TOTAL COGS:	

Price	−	COGS	=	Gross Profit
____________	−	____________	=	____________

IV. Bookkeeping and Financial Analysis/Viability

The traditional internal financial management process consists of four steps:

1. Generate historic, income statement (aka P&L), balance sheet (assets versus liabilities), and statement of cash flows (how would changes in income and balance sheet affect cash?).
2. Forecast income, expenses, and capital expenditures.
3. Generate pro forma, that is, predicted, income statement, balance sheet, and statement of cash flows.

4. Conduct an ongoing analysis of financial results (conducting ratio analyses, measuring results versus plans, and measuring results versus industry norms.)

As a new venture, Step 2 above is the place to start and engaging in regular financial analysis is key. This analysis will give you a sense of how efficiently you are using your assets, how your growth and net profits compare to those of industry peers, where funds needed for capital improvements would come from, possibly ways to partner with other firms to share risk and reduce the amount of cash needed. Finally, the analysis helps address the question of how well the new firm is doing financially.

-Exercise 9.5-

Break-even Analysis. Now that you have a good estimate of the pricing, costs, and gross margin per unit of the product or service you can very easily calculate the break-even point, which is the point at which all costs (fixed and variable) are equal to the sales generated in a given period. Put differently, the break-even point represents the total number of units that must be sold to cover all your expenses. Use the information from the preceding exercises and follow the directions below to calculate your break-even point.

Total Fixed Costs ÷ **Gross Profit** = **Breakeven # of Units**

__________ ÷ __________ = __________

-Exercise 9.6-

Beginning Pro Forma. Now you have just about all of the information you need to start generating some basic financial projections. The only additional information required is a reasonable estimate about the total amount of units that will be sold during a given period. As for the period of time let's use 1 month as the typical time period for basic financial projections/forecasts.

How many sales will you generate in an average month? ___________

Total number of sales × Price per Unit = Total Revenue

___________ × ___________ = ___________

Now net income for the period (1 month) can easily be calculated. All you need to do is calculate the Total COGS (i.e., COGS x number of units sold) and use the following calculation:

Total Revenue − Total COGS − Fixed Costs = Net Income

___________ − ___________ − ___________ = ___________

Hopefully the result is reasonable and attractive. Otherwise, you may need to reconsider various facets of your business model. Also, typically these calculations and presentations would be conducted and presented only once and transferred to a nicely organized and automatically functioning spreadsheet (e.g., Excel). Once you have 1 month's calculations, it's relatively easy to generate the following months and years if you have developed a reasonable set of assumptions (e.g., changes in growth, expenses, and other financials).

Discussion: How easy is it for you to come up with some hard numbers that address revenues and expenses? What if some of the numbers are incorrect or fluctuate? Do you have the resources to undertake the financial management of the firm? Will you need outside advisors or need to hire a professional services firm to assist? What is the most confusing or ambiguous element of this phase?

-Key Points-

– Once you have these projections in a spreadsheet consider how different outcomes and different variables will influence the business's performance. What if you sell less than expected?

What if you change price? Or, if you reduce costs? And so on. It can be difficult to predict sales so be prepared for unexpected outcomes.

- Consider using LivePlan software's financial modeling tool to develop a more comprehensive set of financials and conducting additional modeling (Liveplan.com).
- Financial projections are approximate and estimates by definition. Once the business is operational, financial management and accounting should be *exact!*

Appendix 9

How New Solo Entrepreneurs Can Think Through Their Finances: In this article, you will find helpful tools on how to manage money during a new venture.

https://familybusiness.org/content/How-new-solo-entrepreneurs-can-think-through-the

4 Effective Business Models That Built Billion-Dollar Companies: In this article you will find a helpful roadmap on where your venture will take you.

https://www.entrepreneur.com/article/315056

Why Diversifying Business Revenue Streams Is Crucial to Your Success (And How to Do It): This article will help you avoid vulnerability when revenue is flowing in so that your income stream doesn't dry up and what to do if that does happen.

https://www.entrepreneur.com/article/325941

How to Better Manage Your Cash Flow: In this article you will learn how to improve your receivables, manage payables, and survive your shortfalls.

https://www.entrepreneur.com/article/66008

10 Expert Tips on Managing Cash Flow as a New Business: In this article you will learn about the importance of smart spending along with, when you will break even, how to keep an eye on cash flow management, how to maintain your cash reserve, and much more.

https://www.entrepreneur.com/article/275813

PHASE 10

Putting It All Together and Pitching

I. Validating the Entire Business Model

-Presentation/interactive-

Ideally while completing and working through the various sections of the business model throughout this workbook and associated training you have been speaking to many customers and other stakeholders as well (e.g., partners, suppliers) in an attempt to validate your assumptions and hypotheses about the various components of the business model.

Perhaps the most important attribute of the business model as presented here is that every internal component of the business must fit with the external components (e.g., the market). For example, what if–while calculating the break-even point in the preceding section–the number of units you would need to sell to break even seemed too high (i.e., many more units than you predict you can actually sell)? In theory, you could simply raise the price significantly, then you could break even while selling significantly less units. However, if your customers don't approve of the higher price, you will probably sell even less units than initially

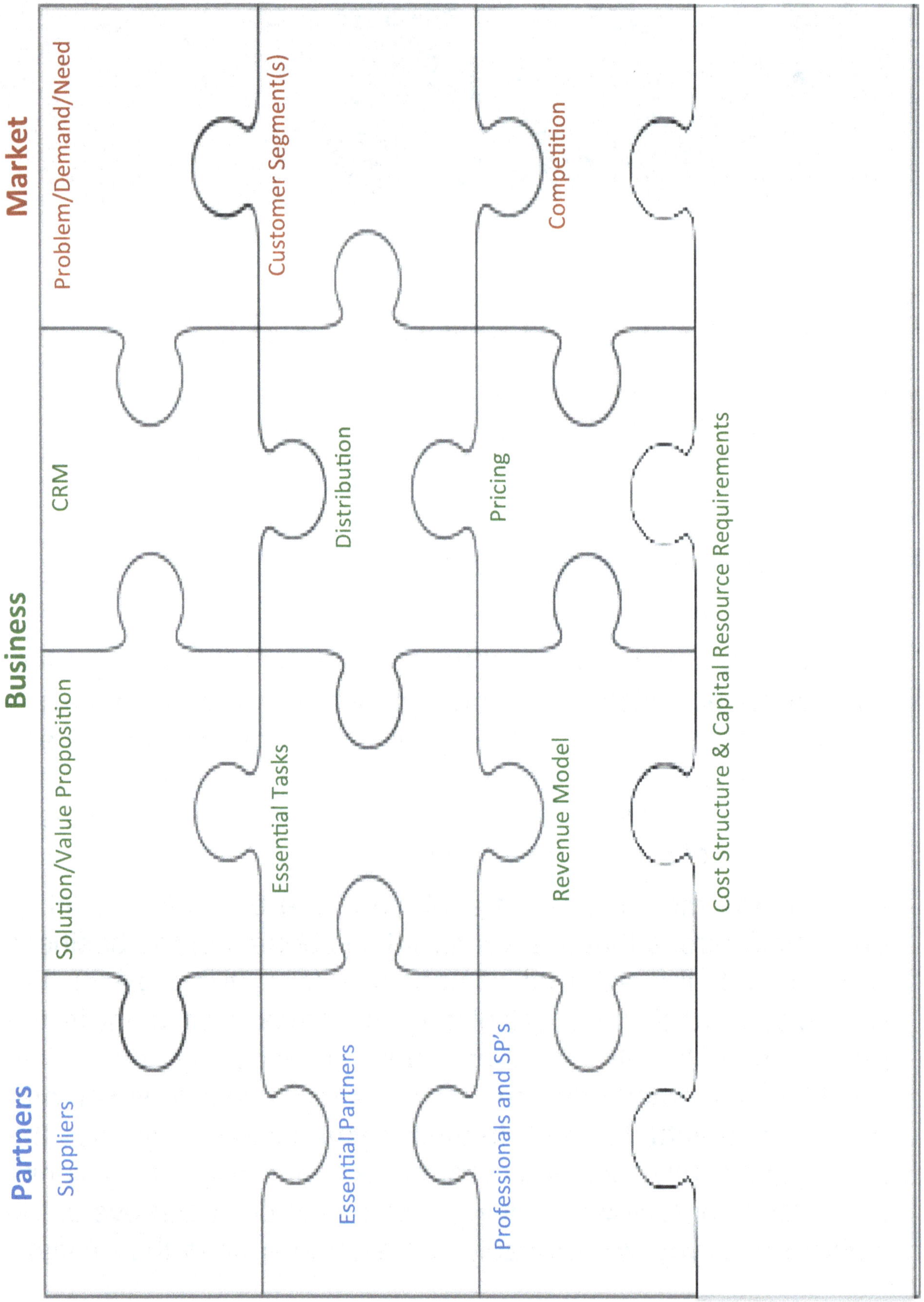

Source: Kevin Cox

predicted, or worse have no sales at all. This is just one example, but remember all of the components of the model must fit with one another and must be empirically validated

-Exercise 10.1-

Assessing the entire business model. Share your business model with the participant nearest to you, allow them to evaluate its validity, ask questions, and offer suggestions. Conduct the same evaluation of that participant's complete business model. Highlight and share two to five attractive and validated business models with the class for discussion.

II. Developing A Pitch

-Presentation/interactive-

Whether you are attempting to convert a customer, win a pitch competition, or attract and convince investors, you will need to develop a great business pitch for your business venture. This is a relatively simple exercise, yet, is often done poorly in practice. It is disappointing because a poor pitch can make a great business model and a great opportunity appear unattractive. Below are some basic instructions for developing a 5- or 10-minute pitch; these instructions are derived largely from the suggestions of one of the most widely known and successful venture capital firms on the planet. Also, while 5 minutes may seem short, it should be more than enough time for you to clearly present your business venture. Also, you will rarely be afforded much more time than that on an initial pitch to an investor or as a contestant in a pitch competition. Approximate times for each section are included and refer to either the shorter or longer version of a pitch. Also, this format is most suited for the traditional pitch competition or attempting to raise funds from investors. If the goal is to convert customers, the pitch may be much shorter and simpler and should focus only on the first four points below.

1. Introduce yourself (name and title) and your business (name) (a few seconds)

2. Present the problem you are solving (i.e., customer problem); this should be clear and compelling (either 30 seconds or 60 seconds)
3. Present your product/service. This should be accomplished in one to two sentences maximum (15 seconds or 30 seconds)
4. Present your advantage versus the competition (15 seconds or 30 seconds)
5. Market size and revenue model. Who will pay for the product (target market), how much will they pay, how will they pay? Convey a deep and comprehensive understanding of the market. Explain what they are paying for and how customers are converted. (60 seconds or 90 seconds)
6. Present your current status and any key metrics for the business. Explain when the company was founded, the current stage of development, how many customers you have, users, revenue, or any other meaningful metrics for the business. (15 seconds or 30 seconds)
7. Present the management team, key members' backgrounds, experience, and current role. (30 seconds or 60 seconds)
8. Present the funds required. How much is the company attempting to raise? And how will the money will be spent to grow the business? (30 seconds or 60 seconds)
9. Present 3-year projections and include the essential assumptions that underlie the model, make sure the model is logical and defensible. (60 seconds or 90 seconds)
10. Thank the audience and offer to answer any questions.

-Exercise 10.2-

Constructing your pitch. Applying the outline provided in the last section, use the 10 boxes below to sketch out a draft of content for a 5-minute pitch. Once complete, pitch your business to the group in no more than 5 minutes.

Discussion: What attributes characterized the most effective pitches, and why? How might the pitches be improved? Are there any other notable issues, concerns, or ideas?

III. Executing a Pitch

Executing a pitch is nothing more than public speaking and nailing any type of presentation. As such the very same rules, tips, suggestions, and advice apply along with a few context-specific details. Your instructor should be able to provide a general overview of things to do and things to avoid. Also see Appendix 10 for additional resources.

IV. Additional Considerations

There are an immense amount of additional issues, information, challenges, decisions, and considerations to think about when starting a business that are not explicitly covered throughout this training program. This is framework, which—if used properly—can determine and even develop a viable business model. However, once you have a business model that is validated and worth pursuing, there are a whole host of additional considerations. For example:

- Can you, and/or should you, raise outside funds? (see Special Topics in Entrepreneurship 1).

- Should you protect any intellectual property? (see Special Topics in Entrepreneurship 2).
- What type of legal entity should be used to organize your business? (see Special Topics in Entrepreneurship 3).
- What types of licenses and permits and other regulatory issues must you consider? (see Special Topics in Entrepreneurship 4).
- Should I franchise my new venture or become a franchisee of an existing business? (see Special Topics in Entrepreneurship 5).

Appendix 10

Y Combinator's advice on how to pitch to investors.

http://paulgraham.com/investors.html

Y Combinator's advice on how to develop a pitch.

https://vator.tv/news/2010-12-14-how-to-write-a-killer-deck-and-get-funded

Special Topics in Entrepreneurship (STE)

STE 1 New Venture Finance: Debt, Equity, and Bootstrapping

I. Essentials of Financing Start-up and Growth Costs

-Reading-

As you investigate starting your new venture and map out potential start-up costs and operational expenses, it is a good idea to consider the two main sources of start-up capital beyond your own resources: **Debt financing** and **equity investment.**

Debt Financing

Debt financing involves two main alternatives: loans from banks or from individuals. Banks require secured debt or personal guarantees. You can use your own property as collateral for the debt or other means. The main goal of the bank is repayment of the debt plus interest. Banks are cash flow lenders; they want assurance that the borrower has cash flow to repay the debt. Unfortunately, many new ventures have limited cash flow. Individuals may make loans to the new venture and seek repayment either via company revenues or a note that is convertible to part ownership in the new venture. Take care with debt: New ventures have high risk and may take longer and be more expensive to develop. Banks operate on low margins; they want to be paid back. A line of credit (similar to a credit card) with a bank is a good plan to cover emergency cash flow needs, particularly if your new venture relies on seasonal revenue.

Equity Investment

You may seek investors who will gain a percentage of ownership in the new venture in exchange for their investment. This investment may come from early stage investors, who are usually **relationship** investors; sometimes termed friends, family (and fools). **High Net Worth Individuals** ($1 million in assets or $300,000 in yearly income) may be approached for investment but many nascent entrepreneurs do not know any high net worth investors. If you do not know any high net worth individuals, it will be *very hard* to raise money. The entrepreneur should beware of investors you do not know; and individuals who are not high net worth. Always work with an attorney, and worry about getting sued for misleading the investors (be up-front and detailed about risk factors). Keep investors informed; do not hype the deal; tell them about bad things that could happen, that is, they could lose their money if financial forecasts aren't realized!

New venture entrepreneurs generally have limited access to **Institutional Investors.** However, a growing venture that has demonstrated cash flow may attract funding from **Angel Groups** (these are sometimes a fund; sometimes a collection of individuals; sometimes they are individuals who want to invest and become active in advising the company as they may have entrepreneurial or industry expertise). **Venture Capitalists** are later stage investors; they like to have complete management teams in place, ongoing sales, and potential for high growth; one in ten of the companies they invest in is considered home run investment. They tend to exert more control on the company and take more equity in exchange for their capital; control that some entrepreneurs are not comfortable giving up. Finally, **Corporate Partners** may have funds to invest but they also bring value (e.g., sales expertise, or market access) in addition to money. They may be great allies if you have intellectual property.

Discussion: What do you believe is the most feasible type of financing you can obtain for your new venture? Is it debt, equity, or a combination? What sources are most available to you?

II. Bootstrapping as an Alternative to Debt and Equity: The Essentials

Bootstrapping is a process of growing a new venture through cash flow. It is a strategy for new companies to access resources when external investors and/or debt financing are limited. The entrepreneur grows the new venture through his/her own assets, selling something from the beginning, and taking as little money as possible out of the business. Whether it is a feasible strategy depends on the type of business and the situation.

In the pre-start-up phase, the entrepreneur should design a business model that keeps expenses low and saves cash. The entrepreneur should not quit the day job too soon. Try to sell something before quitting the job. An initial contract can kick off the company. You should try to develop the product/service before start-up, and get your personal financial position in order: Refinance your house; pay off credit cards, and obtain cash. You want to be able to survive and pull as little money as possible out of the business. You should also avoid debt: Do not put your house up as collateral.

In the start-up phase, Sell!!! If your product/service is not ready, then sell something else. Develop cash flow and keep it moving. Do not ***buy*** any assets like a truck or equipment: these are easy to buy, and hard to sell. Lease or rent instead. Get credit/terms from vendors/suppliers.

To bootstrap operations, hire students or part-time workers, use contractors (e.g., pay them when you're paid), offer stock options for key employees, and consider other options that will keep salaries low. Pay no bill before the due date and if you run behind on cash, then call and negotiate with the vendor to pay something. When you are getting paid for your product or service, take credit cards to bring money in faster, invoice as soon as you can, get money up front and via periodic payments, and collect your receivables as quickly as possible—don't wait. If a customer owes you money, do not sell them anything else until you are paid. Get a small credit line as soon as possible and use it to cover cash flow shortfalls. Pay off the credit line when due so as to avoid interest payments.

-Exercise STE 1-

Consider your new venture and your personal situation. List all of the potential ways that you could bootstrap your venture.

Pre-start-up

____

____

____

____

Start-up

____

____

____

____

Operations

____

____

____

____

Discussion: Advantages of Bootstrapping. Bootstrapping forces you to focus on sales and customer needs. When you are successful, you still own everything. For many entrepreneurs, it is the only way you can start your business. If the business does not work as planned, then shut it down and get a job. As you have not borrowed money, you do not go bankrupt and you do not lose your house. Wait a couple of years, and make a comeback: Tenacity in the face of failure is key to an entrepreneur's success.

Questions?

-Presentation/interactive-

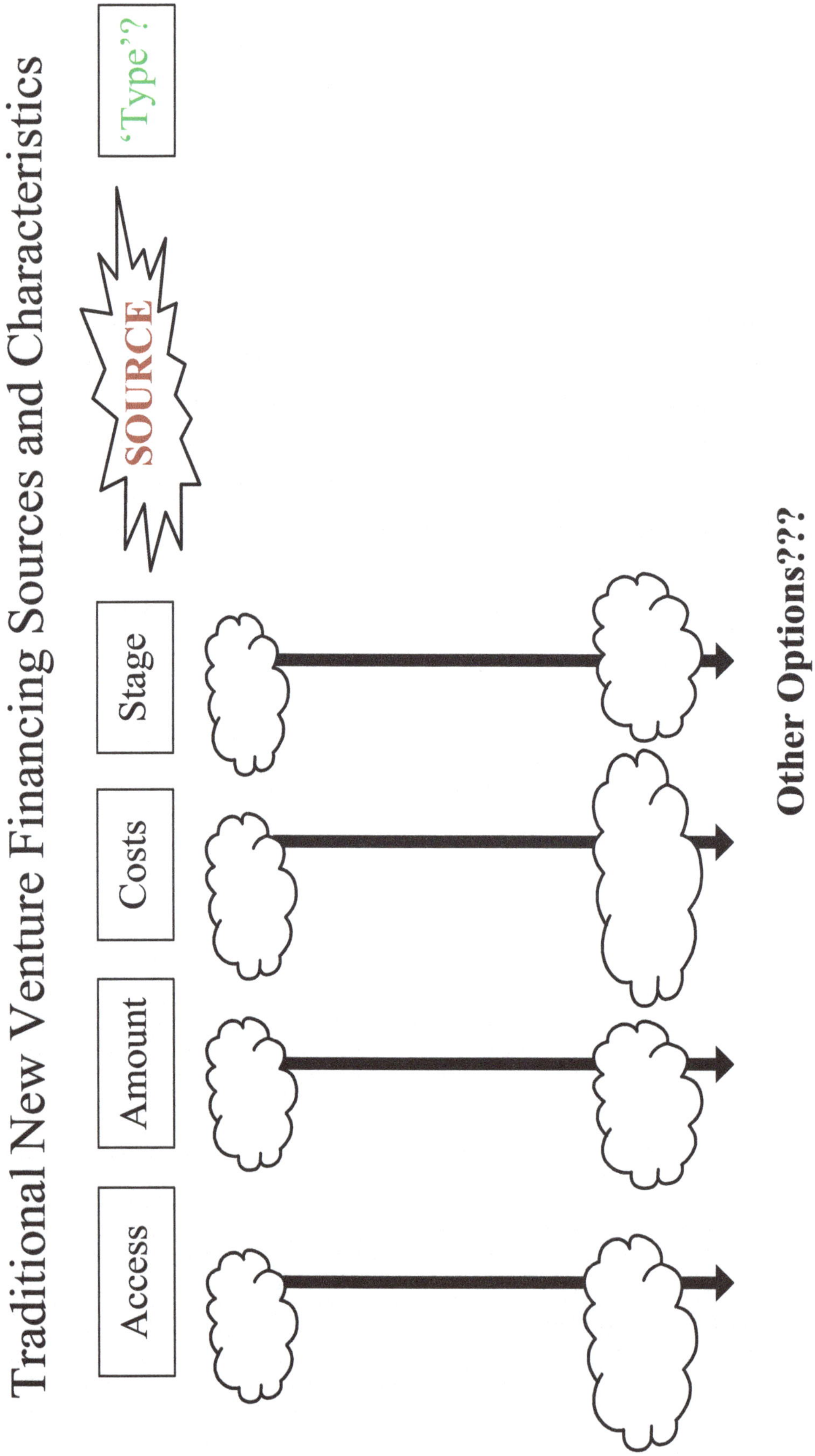

Source: Kevin Cox

III. Nontraditional or Alternative Funding Sources and Strategies

Crowdfunding has burst onto the new venture financing scene as a viable option to fund start-ups without needing to rely on traditional equity or debt finance. Crowdfunding refers to raising capital through the collective effort of friends, family, individual investors, and most commonly customers. While there are a myriad of different types of crowd funding, by far the most widely used and popular for new venture financing is reward-based crowdfunding. This methodology is essentially utilizing presales of your product directly to customers to fund the initial production, which is then delivered to those customers sometime after the campaign. You are likely familiar with one or both of the largest platforms: Kickstarter and Indiegogo. As mentioned, there are other types of crowdfunding such as donation (Gofundme), debt (Lending Club), equity (SeedInvest), or even real estate and royalties from sales. Some crowdfunding campaigns even cater to very specific industries (e.g., Barnraiser). Many features of crowdfunding make it attractive for entrepreneurs.

However, along with the increased popularity, the competition for dollars on crowdfunding campaigns has drastically intensified and now you will need a *really* great product, *really* great video, and some mechanism to drive traffic to your campaign without spending too much money (i.e., more than you are going to make from the campaign). Additionally, reward-based crowdfunding is not a viable option for all business ventures, and success rates vary considerably across categories/industries. For example, most services cannot be crowdfunded using presales ("rewards") because it's impossible to easily deliver a service across the country or around the world.

This website categorizes, rates, and describes most available crowdfunding platforms.

http://crowdsunite.com/

This article provides additional information about crowdfunding and links to additional resources.

https://www.entrepreneur.com/article/228125

This article provides some insights into challenges with crowdfunding.

https://eiexchange.com/content/141-when-kickstarter-campaigns-dont-deliver-a-case-s?search=

Competitions have now become so widespread that they represent a viable option for financing the early stages of a new venture. There are countless local, national, and international business plan/pitch competitions that have cash and/or in-kind prizes. Hitting the competition circuit is particularly viable and attractive for students (at any level) because many competitions only allow students or recent graduates to compete. Luckily there are many other competitions that allow any entrepreneur to participate. In most cases, the prizes are no strings attached, meaning you do not have to give up any equity (ownership) you simply receive the funds in the form of a grant. Business plan and pitch competitions also often have the added benefit of providing important and helpful feedback and direction from judges, and providing participants with valuable experience they will need if they intend to pitch to investors at some point. One warning or potential downside about pitch competitions is that there are so many that entrepreneurs can get preoccupied with competing in all of the competitions to such an extent they do not reserve sufficient time or other resources to actually build the business and instead simply keep honing the pitch—don't forget to keep building the business!

BUSINESS INCUBATORS and **Business Accelerators** are closely related to competitions, as most hold some type of competition to determine who is accepted into the accelerator. The most successful and wildly known example is the Y Combinator, but there are now many of these throughout the United States, some associated with universities, others associated with other public entities (e.g., economic development initiatives), nonprofits, and private sector. If you are accepted into an incubator or accelerator, make sure you conduct sufficient due diligence prior to committing involvement.

Purchase Order Financing is also a viable option for certain entrepreneurs/businesses. Purchase order financing is for businesses that do not have the cash or the inventory required to fulfill and complete customer orders (but they have the purchase order in hand from the customer). There are two options you choose from in purchase order financing. First, the purchase order finance company will collect the invoice from the end customer. The purchase order finance company then makes its money by charging the company in need of funds and various fees. These fees are from the collected invoice. The finance company return the remaining amount to the company. The second option is for the purchase order financing company to open a line of credit with the supplier. The line of credit will be opened in its name and backed by the financing company. With a line of credit, businesses with poor credit or few assets get the supplies they need. This can be a very attractive option in certain situations (e.g., large orders from entities with good credit).

Grants are another way to fund certain types of businesses. Two of the more common, and consistently available, grants are the **Small Business Innovation Research** (SBIR) and **The Small Business Technology Transfer** (STTR). **SBIR** grant program is a highly competitive program that encourages domestic small businesses to engage in Federal Research/Research and Development (R/R&D) that has the potential for commercialization. Through a competitive awards-based program, SBIR enables small businesses to explore their technological potential and provides the incentive to profit from its commercialization. By including qualified small businesses in the nation's R&D arena, high-tech innovation is stimulated and the United States gains entrepreneurial spirit as it meets its specific research and development (R&D) needs. **STTR** is another grant program that expands funding opportunities in the federal innovation R&D arena. Central to the program is expansion of the public/private sector partnership to include the joint venture opportunities for small businesses and nonprofit research institutions. The unique feature of the STTR program is the requirement for the small business to formally collaborate with a research institution in Phase I and Phase II. STTR's most important role is to bridge the gap between performance of basic science and commercialization of resulting innovations. There are many additional grant program both publicly and privately funded. There are countless opportunities but only certain grants will be appropriate/fit with certain business ventures and technologies.

STE 2 Intellectual Property

-Reading-

There are five types of intellectual property, each of which may be more or less important for your business. If you consider any, or multiple types of intellectual property essential for the success of your business you should consider speaking to a qualified attorney. Only a summarized overview of each is provided here.

Trademarks refer to word, phrase, symbol, or design, or a combination, that identifies and distinguishes the source of the goods (e.g., company logo). Service marks are the same as a trademark, except that they identify and distinguish the source of a service rather than goods. Trademarks protect consumers by preventing mistakes, confusion, or deception and simultaneously preserve market reputation for those producing the goods. Trademarks also serve as guarantees of quality and valuable marketing and advertising mechanisms.

Patents are intellectual property rights granted by the government of a nation to an inventor that gives them the exclusive right to the invention for up to 20 years, in exchange for disclosing the details of the new technology to the public for its benefit. The right conferred by the patent grant is, in the language of the statute and of the grant itself, "the right to exclude others from making, using, offering for sale, or selling" the invention in the United States or "importing" the invention into the United States (rights will vary across countries). What is granted is not the right to make, use, offer for sale, sell or import, but the right to exclude others from making, using, offering for sale, selling or importing the invention. Once a patent is issued, the patentee must enforce the patent without aid of the U.S. Patent and Trademark Office. Anything that is deemed new, useful, and nonobvious machine, process, manufacture, or composition can potentially be patented. There are three distinctive types of patents:

1. **Utility patents** may be granted to anyone who invents or discovers any new and useful process, machine, article of manufacture, or composition of matter, or any new and useful improvement thereof;
2. **Design patents** may be granted to anyone who invents a new, original, and ornamental design for an article of manufacture; and
3. **Plant patents** may be granted to anyone who invents or discovers and asexually reproduces any distinct and new variety of plant.

Patents can be extremely valuable, or completely worthless, what is more important is developing something in demand. Patents can also be expensive and time consuming to acquire and other protections may be more important when compared to intellectual property. For example, the founder of Ring (Doorbell Company) opted not to pursue patents and instead focused on speed and being first to market; this strategy proved effective as the company was sold to Amazon for $1 billion.

Copyrights protect all the books, music, research, and all other forms of creative work produced in the United States (policies will vary by country). Copyrights protect the authors of "original works of authorship" fixed in any tangible medium of expression. The manner and medium of fixation are virtually unlimited. Creative expression may be captured in words, numbers, notes, sounds, pictures, or any other graphic or symbolic media.The subject matter of copyright is extremely broad, including literary, dramatic, musical, artistic, audiovisual, and architectural works. Copyright protection is available to both published and unpublished works. Although it is often unknown about copyrights, according to the USPTO, "no publication, registration or other action in the Copyright Office is required to secure copyright. Copyright is secured automatically when the work is created, and a work is 'created' when it is fixed in a "copy or a phonorecord for the first time." Understanding and protecting copyrights can be essential for writers, editors, publishers, and other small business owners.

Trade Secrets can be viewed as an alternative to patent or trademark intellectual property law; both patents and trademarks require public disclosure, whereas trade secrets require the opposite—meaning they are not to be publicly disclosed and are instead to be kept secret. Trade secrets consist of information and can include a formula, pattern, compilation, program, device, method, technique, or process (i.e., almost anything of value). To meet the most common and fundamental requirement, a trade secret must be used in business, and provide an opportunity to obtain an economic advantage over competitors who do not know it or use it. One benefit of a trade secret is that the lifespan is indefinite, and *potentially* unlimited unlike a patent. However, if the secret is revealed, or figured out by someone else, you are not afforded any protection, or exclusive rights at all. As such trade secrets are better for some processes (e.g., things that are nearly impossible to reverse engineer, or figure out; algorithms and recipes) and not well suited for others (e.g., things that are easily reverse engineered, or easy to figure out; hardware).

Contracts, although part of a much broader area of law, also sometimes take the form of intellectual property and therefore represent the fifth and final type of intellectual property. A contract agreement might be established to allow only a certain vendor in a certain location or territory, thereby excluding others. For example, most universities only have available Coca-Cola or PepsiCo products across the entire campus; this is due to a (potentially very large) contract agreement.

The following link provides free resources and guidance related to intellectual property.

https://michelsonip.com/

United States Patent and Trademark Office provides much more information and resources about intellectual property.

https://www.uspto.gov/

https://www.uspto.gov/learning-and-resources/inventors-entrepreneurs-resources

STE 3 Legal Forms of Business

-Reading-

I. Overview of Common Legal Forms of Business and Practical Advice

The most common and easiest form of business to set up in the United States is by far a **Sole Proprietorship** (and to a lesser extent, a **Partnership**). There's no fee and no filing. Essentially, you simply start doing business, and in the case of partnership you're not required to have any filing or paperwork either, but you're strongly advised to create a partnership agreement. However, there is one clear and major downside to both of these legal entities, the owner(s) have personal liability for the business, meaning if you have some legal issue your personal assets can be in jeopardy, which may be untenable for most people/business owners.

In many cases, when initially starting a business, the easiest and safest choice of legal form is a **Limited Liability Company** (or **LLC**). These can be set up as single member (one owner) or multiple (similar to a partnership with shared ownership). This entity is very easy to create, (e.g., in the state of Florida, documents can easily be filed electronically at sunbiz.org) and also inexpensive – between $100 and $200 if you do it yourself. An LLC is not always the right choice depending on the business, but often it is. Other legal forms of business include **S Corporations, C corporations, Limited Partnerships (LP), and Limited Liability Partnership (LLP), and Non-profit**. Section II provides an overview of the basic characteristics of each. Many states also now have a legal form such as **Benefit Corporation** (or similar name/designation) designed to specifically suit social entrepreneurship enterprises (See STE 7 for more details).

II. Quick Guide for Legal Form Characteristics

-Reference-

	Sole Proprietorship	General Partnership	LLC	Limited Partnership	Limited Liability Partnership	S Corporation	C Corporation
State filing and fee required	No	No	Yes	Yes	Yes	Yes	Yes
Ongoing state filing fees	No	No	Yes	Yes	Yes	Yes	Yes
Limited liability protection	No	No	Yes	Varies	Yes	Yes	Yes
Unlimited duration	No	No	Varies	Yes	Varies	Yes	Yes
Strict corporate requirements	No	No	No	No	No	Yes	Yes
Flexible management changes	No	No	Yes	No	Yes	No	No
Business taxed at entity level	No	No	Varies	No	No	No	Yes
Pass through income/loss	Yes	Yes	Yes	Yes	Yes	Yes	No
Double taxation	No	No	No	No	No	No	Yes
Ease of raising capital	No	No	Varies	No	No	Yes	Yes
Ease of transferring ownership	No	No	Varies	Varies	Varies	Yes	Yes

STE 4 Regulatory Issues

-Reading-

Finishing up the law/legal special topics in entrepreneurship, most businesses have to deal with some types of regulatory issues. These can take many forms including but not limited to: **licenses, authorizations, technical specifications, safety specifications, inspections, permits, environmental regulations, legal limits or constraints, and others**.

These considerations vary infinitely based on the type of business and specific location and cannot all possibly be covered here. Instead, it is important that you know what regulatory issues are relevant to your business and within your industry. This information is generally publicly available but may not always be easy to find. You may prefer to get help or legal guidance in this area; owners of the same type of business can also provide considerable insight and may be less expensive or free.

Another source to obtain information and advice about regulatory issues as well as legal forms of business and other matters is the local office of the Small Business Development Center, an agency of the U.S. Small Business Administration.

https://americassbdc.org/

STE 5 Franchising

-Reading-

Franchising is a form of business organization in which a firm that already has a successful product or service (franchisor) licenses its trademark and method of doing business to another business or individual (franchisee) in exchange for a franchise fee and an ongoing royalty payment. There are two types of franchise systems:

1. **Business Format Franchise** is an arrangement under which the franchisor provides a formula for doing business to the franchisee along with training, advertising, and other forms of assistance. Fast food restaurants, convenience stores, and motels are well-known examples of business format franchises. Business format franchises are by far the most popular form of franchising, particularly for entrepreneurial firms.
2. **Product and Trademark Franchise** is an arrangement under which the franchisor grants to the franchisee the right to buy its products and use its trade name. This approach typically connects a single manufacturer with a network of dealers or distributors. For example, General Motors has established a network of dealers that sell GM cars and use the GM trademark in their advertising and promotions. Other examples of product and trademark franchisors include agricultural machinery dealers, soft drink bottlers, and beer distributorships.

I. Franchising Your Business

Establishing a franchise system should be approached carefully, deliberately, and with caution. Franchising is a complicated business endeavor, and entrepreneurs must look closely at all its aspects before deciding to franchise. Entrepreneurs should also be aware that over the years a number of fraudulent franchise organizations have come and gone and have left financially ruined franchise owners behind. Franchising is most appropriate when a firm has a strong or potentially strong trademark, a well-designed business method, and a desire to grow. A franchise system will ultimately fail if the franchisor's brand doesn't add value for customers and its business method is flawed or poorly developed.

Potential Benefits: Rapid, low-cost market expansion, income from franchise fees and royalties, franchisee motivation, access to ideas and suggestions, cost savings, increased buying power

Potential Disadvantages: Profit sharing, loss of control, friction with franchisees, managing growth, differences in required business skills, legal expenses

II. Buying a Franchise to Operate as Franchisee

Purchasing a franchise is an important business decision involving a substantial financial commitment. Potential franchise owners should strive to be as well informed as possible before purchasing a franchise and should be aware that it is often legally and financially difficult to exit a franchise relationship. There are a number of costs involved with buying a franchise that should be considered.

1. Initial Franchise Fee—The initial fee varies depending on the franchisor.
2. Capital Requirements—The costs vary but may include the cost of buying real estate, the cost of putting up a building, the purchase of inventory, and the cost of obtaining a business license.
3. Continuing Royalty Payment—Usually around 5% of monthly gross income.
4. Advertising Fees—Franchisees often required to pay into national or regional advertising funds.
5. Other Fees—these may include training staff, providing management expertise as needed, computer assistance, and a wide array of other support items.

Potential Benefits: A proven product or service within an established market, an established trademark or business system, franchisor's training, technical expertise, and managerial expertise, an established marketing network, franchisor ongoing support, availability of financing, potential for business growth.

Potential Disadvantages: Cost of the franchise, restrictions on creativity, duration and nature of the commitment, risk of fraud, misunderstandings, or lack of franchisor commitment, problems of termination or transfer, poor performance on the part of other franchisees, potential for failure.

III. Legal Aspects of the Franchise Relationship

The offer and sale of a franchise are regulated at the federal level via a Franchise Disclosure Document. According to Federal Trade Commission (FTC) rule 436, franchisors must furnish potential franchisees with written disclosures that provide information about the franchisor, the franchised business, and the franchise relationship. In most cases, the disclosures are made through a lengthy document referred to as the Franchisor Disclosure Document (FDD). The FDD contains 23 categories of information that give a prospective franchisee a broad base of information about the background and financial health of the franchisor.

The majority of franchisors and franchisees are highly ethical. There are certain features of franchising, however, that make it subject to ethical abuse. These features are as follows: the get-rich-quick mentality, the false assumption that buying a franchise is a guarantee of business success, and conflicts of interest between franchisors and franchisees.

IV. International Franchising

International opportunities for franchising are becoming more prevalent for the following two reasons: (1) The markets for certain franchised products in the United States have become saturated (e.g., fast food), and (2) The trend toward globalization continues.

Steps to take before buying a franchise overseas: Consider the value of the franchisor's name in the foreign country, get a good lawyer, determine whether the product or service is salable in the foreign country, find out how much training and support you will receive from the franchisor.

This is a link to an article about assessing and selecting franchises.

https://www.entrepreneur.com/encyclopedia/franchising

This website provides a great deal of information about potential franchise opportunities:

https://www.franchise.org/

Shrimp Tank Podcast: This interview with Maximo Cortese of the Poke Company provides information about a nascent franchise operation in the fast-casual restaurant segment.

https://shrimptankpodcast.com/boca-raton-episode-67-maximo-cortese-co-founder-of-the-poke-company/

STE 6 Website Considerations for Startups

-Reading-

I. Introduction

There are three main components every business will need in order to put its company on the web. First is a host, second is a content management system, and third is a domain. Thankfully, modern-day web development is much simpler than what it was 10 or 20 years ago. Anyone who has access to the Internet and a basic ability to edit a word document or slide deck also has the ability to develop and launch their own website. The good news is that all of this can be done relatively quickly and cheaply. The three things mentioned above are often readily available from one or two major sources. We will go through each element one-by-one here.

People are commonly intimidated when they hear about these types of things needed for a website, but really they are pretty straightforward. A host is nothing more than a company that provides you with a computer that will store all your website's files and make them available to the internet 24/7 so your customer can always access it. A content management system, or CMS, is software that allows you to manage the content of your website. This is where advances have made web development accessible to anyone with CMSs that work as What You See Is What You Get (WYSIWYG) editors. In essence, it is often times completely unnecessary to look at any code to develop a website as CMSs work like word processors or PowerPoint with drag and drop functionality. Finally, a domain is just the letters that customers will type into their web browser to access your website.

What Is Your Customer Trying to Do?

The major decision that needs to be made is the type of website your company will need. Specifically, this will largely depend on three things your customer might be coming to your website for. First, if your customer is simply trying to learn more about your company, product, or service (think of a local restaurant that might present its hours of operation and menu), then a basic informational/content website will suffice. These websites are made up of text, image, and video content that give customers the information about the company they are looking for. These are the most basic and easiest of websites to put together.

The second thing your customer might be trying to do is buy something from your company on your website. You might think of going to Nike's website and selecting a new pair of shoes that you will purchase on their site to have sent to you. For these types of companies, they will require the same type of informational/content website from earlier along with e-commerce abilities like shopping carts, product pages, and the ability to process credit card transactions directly on the site.

Finally, if your customer is trying to do something beyond the first two behaviors listed above (learn more about your company or buy something from you), then that most likely means that your website is the solution itself that you are presenting to your customer. Think of a company like Airbnb where the website is the solution and the customer is doing more than just learning about Airbnb or trying to buy something. The website itself is a platform that brings together people interested in listing their homes for rent and people looking to rent those homes. The website is the solution for the company and it does more than just present information or make a sale.

II. The Best Providers to Use

Depending on the type of website from above you determine your company will need, the host and CMS provider will be very easy to choose. Let's start with basic informational/content websites. This type of company would need just a simple website builder CMS and there are a lot of providers out there. Wix, GoDaddy, Squarespace, and Google Sites are all options here, but from experience, it seems most students are able to work with Wix the best. Some of the benefits of Wix are:

- Easy to use WYSIWYG editor with drag and drop capabilities and readymade elements
- Ready to go professional-looking templates that allow you to start with a website structure that looks good before you edit a single thing
- Cheap plans and no long-term contract that include both hosting and CMS functionality included
- The ability to start for free

Regardless of whether you go with Wix or another provider listed above, all provide both CMS and hosting packaged together.

For companies looking for e-commerce capabilities, Shopify is the industry leader and was built from the ground up to provide everything a company would need including specialized hosting and a CMS specific for e-commerce. The pros of Shopify are:

- WYSIWYG editor with proven templates specifically designed to drive e-commerce conversions
- Built in merchant processing that allows you to process credit card transactions instantly at a fair price
- A blazing fast worldwide Content Delivery Network that ensures your e-commerce store loads quickly, something incredibly important when it comes to selling on the Internet

- Dynamic mobile pages that ensure your site looks good on both desktops and mobile devices
- A free trial to test out all of the capabilities

There are other providers that will give hosting and CMS capabilities for e-commerce, but Shopify is the provider that was built ground up for the purpose of providing services for e-commerce sites.

Finally, for companies in need of a website that does more than just provide informational content or an e-commerce store, there are more nuanced decisions that will need to be made. Because these types of websites will do more advanced things, these companies will have to look to other providers or potentially outsource to professionals. There are three basic options here:

1. WordPress with a specialized plugin that provides the advanced functionality the company needs. WordPress is an open-source CMS that works well with third-party developers that have created a ton of different plugins that give your site the same WYSIWYG editor functionality described above along with advanced features. For example, if you were looking for a site that had listing features similar to Airbnb, there would be a WordPress plugin that would allow you to create that functionality on your site relatively easily. This might take some searching around to see if there is a plugin out there that does what you need it to do, and it might need some customizing on your part, but WordPress with the right plugin might be a great option for launching an MVP to test basic features.
2. Visual programming providers such as Bubble.io allow users to develop web and mobile apps in a WYSIWYG editor while also providing a backend database and visual programming functionality. These types of softwares allow users to program apps without having to learn or look at code since it is entirely

visual in a point-and-click format. Companies like Bubble.io allow entrepreneurs to develop and launch their web apps quickly and easily at the fraction of the cost of a traditional developer. While there is a learning curve, it is much less than trying to learn traditional code.

3. Hiring a developer or outsourcing to a developer would be the last option for the most complex websites. However, these would most likely fall outside of MVP types of builds and would not be recommended due to the cost and time required. If you are thinking of hiring a developer, it would be strongly recommended that you first investigate the plugins available on WordPress (point 1 above) or the ability to develop your solution on a visual programming software like Bubble.io (point 2 above) before committing the time and money to a custom-built solution.

III. The Final Requirement: A Domain

The providers all listed and recommended above will give you both the hosting and CMS capabilities you will need to get your website up and running. However, the final third element required would be a domain. The good news is that the providers listed above will all often sell you a domain as well and integrate it so you can get your website live easily. However, we would recommend you also look at Google Domains as a provider for your domain services. After buying your domain through Google Domains, it is a very easy process to point that domain at your website that might be hosted with any of the other providers listed above.

When you are looking into your domain, there are some basic considerations. Obviously, you would want it to communicate your company's name and brand as best as possible. However, as you start searching for available domains, you might notice that what you are looking for is not readily available since it might be owned by someone else. In these cases, you might have to look for something else that is close. Generally, you will want to stick with .com Top-Level Domains (TLDs); however .org is appropriate for nonprofits and .net is OK as well. There are some Search Engine Optimization (SEO) considerations for TLDs, and people might look at other TLDs as not as legitimate as a .com, but these are more advanced ideas. Customers seem to be getting more comfortable with industry-specific TLDs like .shop for an e-commerce store. At a minimum, it might be better to find a good .com rather than a great domain with a different TLD.

STE 7 Social Entrepreneurship

-Reading-

Social entrepreneurship is the creation of social impact by developing and implementing a sustainable business model that draws on innovative solutions that benefit society. In a sense, social entrepreneurship is a crossover between strictly for-profit enterprises and nonprofit business entities. Social entrepreneurs pursue both economic and social goals and performance outcomes. Social entrepreneurship has proven capable of having massive and impactful influences on individuals and societies around the world. It's important to highlight that because these entities are not nonprofit, but instead have a retained revenue generating model that can be more sustainable than some nonprofit enterprises.

Two notable examples of social entrepreneurship you might be familiar with are 4Ocean and Toms Shoes. Social entrepreneurship is highlighted here as an option because some entrepreneurs presume that if their primary objective is to help people, or society then they *must* be a nonprofit enterprise, and this is simply not the case. In fact, many business ventures that initially resemble nonprofit organizations have the potential to develop a revenue generating component and should consider social entrepreneurship as a viable option.

What It Means to be a Social Entrepreneur: Community Need and Passion over Profit are argued to be key aspects:

https://www.entrepreneur.com/article/281214

Shrimp Tank Podcast: This interview with Lauren Koff, cofounder of a social enterprise structured as a nonprofit, explores how she and her colleague started and are growing a new venture with a multiple source revenue model.

https://shrimptankpodcast.com/ep-13-lauren-koff-co-founder-of-mindmelody-2/

STE 8 Marketing, Advertising, Branding, and Public Relations

-Reading-

Marketing is generally used as a broad umbrella term, under which a myriad of other activities resides. Marketing is a process that refers to all the business activities a company implements to bring together buyers and sellers for the exchange of products and services. These tactics can include formulating marketing strategies to use in conjunction with other tools. For example, branding, messaging, content, social media, online presence, public relations (PR), advertising, and even market/customer research are considering marketing. Here, we will provide an overview of a few of those tactics and strategies as they are immensely important to your business because they represent the primary mechanism by which potential customers learn about your company.

Advertising is the activity of producing and sharing media content for commercial products and services. Advertising is when an individual or an organization pays to have announcements sent to the public to try and convince potential or existing consumers to buy a product or service. An advertisement is processed through media such as newspapers, posters, television, radio, or the Internet. Advertising is often referred to as **paid media** because organizations are paying to have their message shown to consumers. One way to differentiate between advertising methodologies or channels/context is to distinguish between traditional advertising and new media. **Traditional advertising** generally refers to print ads, mailers, billboards, newspapers, radio, broadcast and cable television, and anything similar. Although often overlooked as older stale options, traditional advertising techniques can be very effective depending on the nature of the business. **New media** generally refers to advertising on the Internet or digital advertising such as Google AdWords, Social media advertising, pay-per-click, retargeting, and many others. One benefit of these online tactics is the ability to track all attributes of performance, as everything is inherently traceable. This means that for digital advertising it is generally very easy to calculate the return of investment (or ROI), which is key for all paid advertising. Being able to calculate the precise value that is returned (e.g., in sales) for each dollar spent makes decision making and, in some cases, substantial growth and expansion very easy. Decisions about advertising can be made "in-house" by you or by hiring an outside firm. Either way, there should be a clear return on investment, or it is not worth making the investment. However, it is worth noting that there is generally some lag between the investment and the return, so be patient, but not too patient.

Branding includes all of the visual and design elements of your company from the logo to the website and many other items that customer, partners, or others may come into contact with (business cards, letterhead, trade show booth). Branding involves a wide assortment of things that your audiences experience and come to expect that create an association between the consumer's ideals and the product, service, or company in general. Consider some of the most widely known brands and what you think about them and expect from them. Some brands now even seemingly have a personality as the brands interact with customer and consumers directly via social media. In the earliest stages of a company the brand/branding is often an extension of the founder/entrepreneur.

PR is a strategic communication process that builds mutually beneficial relationships between organizations and their stakeholders. The main purpose of public relations is to help organizations maintain a positive image in the eye of the public. Those involved in public relations include company stakeholders, customers, clients, employees, local communities, and several other audience members. PR is essentially used to build and maintain a company's reputation. Public relations is often referred to as **earned media** as it cannot generally be easily purchased. Perhaps the best way to explain this sometimes-confusing part of marketing is with a couple of examples. Public relations would be if a newspaper, magazine, or TV news outlet did a (hopefully positive) story about your company as opposed to advertising where you would buy an ad within a newspaper, magazine, or TV show. It can even be as simple as replying to bad reviews on the Internet or angry customers or implementing a plan to increase the number of positive reviews you receive. Again, you can control these initiatives in-house or hire an external firm to handle them for you. Again, the key metric in this area is return on investment.

STE 9 The Entrepreneurial Family Firm

In many instances, an entrepreneur works directly with his or her family to get a new venture off the ground. In fact, four out of five new ventures are started with family involvement. Family members may work together to start the business or family members may fund the new entrepreneurial venture through debt or equity investment. At the very least, the entrepreneur must balance work life with family life considering all of the hours that go into investigating and starting the venture.

Many new ventures do not succeed yet some evolve into strong businesses that are acquired by other companies. Other new ventures start as or become family firms that involve an entrepreneur's spouse, parents, children, and other relatives. These family firms can be very entrepreneurial at the start and continue to be innovative into the next generation. Yet, only about 30% of family enterprises move to a second generation of ownership and only about 30% of those go on to the third generation. We include this appendix in the workbook regarding family firms mainly due to the impact they have on world economies.

About 80% of world's businesses are family firms and these include some familiar names including Walmart, Oracle, Volkswagen, Samsung, Novartis, S.C. Johnson, Chick Fil A, and Koch Industries. Family firms make up 35% of *Fortune* 500 firms and 60% of public firms in USA, and account for a substantial portion of GDP. Forty percent of these firms will face a leadership change in next 5 years.

A family business is a synthesis of:

- **Ownership control** (15%+) by two or more members of a family or a partnership of families
- **Strategic influence** by family members on the management of the firm
- Concern for **family relationships**
- The dream (possibility) of **continuity** across generations
- The **values of family are** reflected in the business

The challenges facing family firms include those that are faced by many new ventures that are attempting to grow. These include creating effective governance structures such as boards of advisors and directors as well as determining strategic direction for growth, continued innovation, and competitive advantage. Family firms must balance the needs of the family with the needs of the business and must determine the most effective means to work with nonfamily employees, and manage conflict among family members on a day to day and on a long-term basis. Finances and human resource issues must be planned through formal processes. Finally, the transition process from generation to generation must focus on building value and stewardship of the firm if it is to continue to the next generation. If these challenges are not met in the entrepreneurial family firm, then the business may be doomed to failure by the third generation. Such a fate is the subject of prophecy and slogan from various countries around the world:

"*Shirtsleeves to shirtsleeves in three generations.*" (USA)

"*The first generation creates, the second inherits, the third destroys.*" (Germany)

"*From peasant shoes to peasant shoes in three generations.*" (China)

"*From the stable to the stars and back again.*" (Italy)

One means to grow any new venture (and family firm) is the formalization of human resource practices. This effort reflects the importance of the human/intellectual capital resources discussed in phase 7. Here are some quick tips:

- Create rules of entry and minimum standards for employment. Do this ***before*** there is a need.
- Never *create* jobs for family members
- Use the same performance standards for family and nonfamily employees
    - Include nonfamily employees in evaluation
    - Use 360-degree anonymous performance appraisals
    - Foster a culture of merit and fairness
- Make the incentive system transparent
- Clearly define roles and responsibilities
- Hold family members accountable for bad behavior
- Create a code of ethics that applies to all
- The family should not ask others to do what it will not do itself
- Family members are subject to defined expectations for education and work experience *before* joining the firm full-time
- Family members do not report to anyone who is related to them by blood or marriage
- Base compensation on market value
- Regular performance review practices are used (360-degree feedback)
- Measurable goals are established, based on feedback, to be used in future performance evaluations

This website, Family Firm Institute, provides useful and practical information to family firms:

https://www.ffi.org/

This website provides a variety of articles and information helpful in launching, managing, and growing an entrepreneurial family firm:

https://www.familybusiness.org/

Shrimp Tank Podcast: This interview with a mother–daughter entrepreneurial team examines a variety of start-up issues that have been discussed in this workbook as well as the intricacies of successfully launching a new company with a family member:

https://shrimptankpodcast.com/boca-raton-episode-78-berioska-sosa-coo-of-aviva-care-pharmacy-ceo-of-royalty-med-spa-and-mirosis-gonzalez-ceo-of-aviva-care-pharmacy/